GW01086944

GOD IN THE NEW WORLD

GOD IN THE NEW WORLD

by

Lloyd Geering

HODDER AND STOUGHTON

First Published April 1968

Reprinted April 1968

SBN: 340 04430 6

Printed in Great Britain for Hodder and Stoughton Limited, St. Paul's House, Warwick Lane, London, E.C.4, by Cox & Wyman Limited, London, Fakenham and Reading

TO
ELAINE

Foreword

(by the Very Rev. J. M. Bates, former Moderator of the General Assembly of the Presbyterian Church of New Zealand)

Has the Christian Church anything relevant to say to modern man in a secular age?

It has. But before its message can be clearly perceived there are some mists of ignorance and misunderstanding to be blown away. The object of this book is to contribute to this process. In particular there are two points on which the Church today must be ready to speak plainly. One concerns the Bible; the other the relation of the Christian faith to the secular scientific outlook.

Far too few Christians understand the real nature of the Bible, yet some knowledge of how it came to be the book we now have in our hands is a necessity for the whole Church in this modern age. For the most part, at the present time the pulpit and the pew are not on the same wavelength in this matter, and it is high time they were.

Then, too, we have to face the question whether there can be any point of contact between the Christian view of things, and the way educated men look at the world and its history today. This book maintains that there can be, and that the message and meaning of Christ crucified applies to human beings, as such, whatever their circumstances. The secularity of the modern world has not made Christ irrelevant; on the contrary it has made his relevance more evident.

This is a book for thinking people to read and talk about.

J. M. BATES

Preface

This book came to be written in the following way. In 1965 the Editor of our church paper *The Outlook* invited me to write an article to be published prior to Reformation Day on Sunday October 31. This article duly appeared under the title, "Is a New Reformation possible?" I drew attention to the Bishop of Woolwich's new paperback called *The New Reformation*, and attempted to sketch the way in which the contemporary world is challenging much of traditional Christianity. As a result, one or two people were stimulated to write to the Editor, either in alarm or in appreciation.

Then he invited me to write something for the Easter, 1966 edition of *The Outlook*. In an article entitled, "What does the Resurrection mean?" I attempted to sketch the difficulties of relating the Resurrection narratives of the New Testament to the kind of world in which we live, and to show that, in spite of these, the Resurrection faith of the church can still have meaning for men who have left behind the world view of the first century. As a focal point for discussion I referred to some words of Professor R. Gregor Smith in his recent book *Secular Christianity*.

This article brought forth a deluge of letters to the Editor, and as it was clear that many people had been disturbed, I set about writing four articles dealing with the main points being raised. These had to do with the differences between knowledge and faith, an examination of the evidence for the historicity of the empty tomb story, the relationship of the church to her doctrinal standards and the way in which the Bible is to be understood and interpreted. These articles appeared in *The Outlook*, and were later in the year published separately in booklet form.

So far the scope of the discussion and interest aroused was just what one might have expected. It was the next stage in the debate which took most of us by surprise. In two or three of the courts of the Presbyterian Church of New Zealand, there was strong concern expressed about the orthodoxy of the 'Resurrection' article, and as soon as this came to the notice of the press, the debate left the confines of Presbyterian Church circles and became a public issue. The original article was published in full in the leading newspapers of the four main cities. Then for some weeks here in New Zealand, 'Resurrection' became the subject of newspaper editorials, magazine articles, radio talks and TV interviews. I received hundreds of letters, some written in anger, some in appreciation. They came from a wide cross-section of the community.

Two things became clear. There is a tremendous gap in viewpoint and understanding between academic theology and popular Christian thought. Some of the issues that theological students have been discussing all this century are hardly known at all by large numbers of devout church members. Secondly it showed that in a day when it is often assumed that theological questions are no longer of general interest, a vital theological problem can become the main subject of conversation in tea-breaks at factory and office, and can lead Christians and non-Christians to talk seriously and honestly with one another about the Christian faith, and often for the first time in years.

It was suggested to me that I should write something at greater length about the issues raised. Although it appeared to me that there was already a wide variety of popular books available for those interested, I accepted the challenge to set down the nature of our present predicament as I see it. The three parts into which this book falls may also be regarded as an attempt to answer these three questions: "Where are we?" "How did we get here?" "Where do we go from here?"

This book is not intended for professional theologians, and should any such chance upon it, I must beg their indulgence for the many generalizations into which I have been forced in the interests of simplicity. Of course, it is not even written by a professional systematic theologian; my own special interest in the Old Testament no doubt shows through all too plainly. The people I am mainly addressing are those who are genuinely wanting to know what to make of Christianity in this new and fast-changing world. Some of them will be looking at the church from within, and some from without. Some perhaps will be sixth-formers, who, after being schooled in the basic sciences, are wondering what to make of this new world in which they must live.

After only a few chapters had been written a second public debate broke out. I had been invited to preach at the opening service of the Victoria University of Wellington. I preached on some words of Ecclesiastes, "he has put eternity into man's mind, yet so that he cannot find out what God has done from the beginning to the end". The press quoted from this sermon the one sentence, "Man has no immortal soul", and immediately there was a public controversy in which Christians and non-Christians vigorously aired their various views about life after death. The original sermon was published in full in several newspapers. The subject of immortality was discussed on radio and TV and this time the public interest spread to Australia.

While no one really wants to upset the peace, or sow seeds of distress let alone bitterness, it is clear that, if the Christian message is going to be heard in today's world, it must be related to that world, and it is also clear that, if Christians speak about the faith with openness and honesty, there are many more than is often imagined, who are ready to listen.

This book was nearly finished when there was published posthumously a booklet written by my former teacher and late colleague, Professor H. H. Rex, entitled, *Did Jesus rise from the dead?* In it he makes this comment, "we live on this side of a rupture which divides the whole history of mankind into two sections; the one extending from the cavemen to the men of the Renaissance, and the other covering this post-Cartesian world of ours. On the surface it may seem preposterous to lump the caveman, Plato, and Michelangelo into one class, and the rest of us into another. And yet, so long as we fail to appreciate the full magnitude of this fact, we have understood very little about the nature of the modern secular world." It is the nature of this rupture which I have been trying to outline in what follows, along with the reasons for it, and the effect of it on the Christian faith.

In the writing of this book I have been greatly indebted to my wife for her never-failing encouragement. The Very Rev. J. M. Bates, the Rev. D. R. Madill, the Rev. T. M. Corkill and my colleague the Rev. Professor F. W. R. Nichol, I wish to thank warmly for their kindness in reading the manuscript and for the suggestions they have made. I am grateful to Mrs. T. Gordon for her care and patience in the typing of the whole manuscript.

Knox College, Lloyd Geering
October 1967

Contents

PART I

The Coming of the New World

CHAPTER I

The New Source of Knowledge

As soon as one begins to think about the basic issues of human existence, one is faced with the question of where to turn to find a trustworthy guide. What is the source of true knowledge? How do we go about increasing our knowledge and finding the answers to our basic questions? Through most of Christian history the Christian has for this purpose turned to the authoritative teaching of the church, and this included the Bible. It was confidently claimed by the church that Christian doctrine provided clear and final answers to the basic questions of life, and by the time of the Middle Ages these had been built into an impressive and unified body of knowledge.

The church's confidence in her teaching rested upon the belief that the body of knowledge, of which she was the appointed guardian, had been revealed by God through the chosen prophets and apostles of ancient times and especially through Jesus, the Son of God. Because this knowledge came from God, it was absolute and final. Nothing could ever contradict it, and man by himself had no way of finding it out for himself. All men were thus dependent upon the heritage of divine revelation which the church preserved from generation to generation.

This understanding of the source of true knowledge was the Christian version of an almost universal attitude in the ancient world. Man has a strong conservative element in him, for it is his ability to conserve and hand on the heritage from the past that has made possible the evolution of man. The ancient human civilizations gradually developed by the conserving and handing on of the knowledge and practices which had proved themselves in the past.

Man's sense of security was closely bound up with the knowledge and patterns of behaviour he inherited from the past. The known way, however unsatisfactory, was always safer than the unknown way. Of course, even in ancient society there was a small amount of change and development going on all the time, but it was so slow that to man himself it was almost imperceptible. If there was any rapid change, it was due to a calamity of a destructive kind, such as war or plague. So change was commonly thought of as evil, and something to be feared.

This in turn led to the commonly-held belief that the golden age of human society lay in the past, and hence true knowledge was to be gained by searching for the best that past ages had bequeathed. That knowledge which had been inherited from time immemorial was readily reverenced as being of divine origin, and was incomparable with anything that could be discovered in the present. Ancient man did not expect any of his contemporaries to surpass the great teachers of the past, and he was greatly suspicious of anything that was new. He expected to find truth in that which was already stamped with the authority of the ages.

While this veneration of the past and suspicion of the new is by no means absent in our world today, it is no longer the dominant attitude of modern man concerning the source of true knowledge. We live in a period of rapid changes of all kinds, and we have come to accept change, development and progress as part of the order of things. We are used to seeing the 'old' being quickly superseded by the 'new', whether it is the automobile, the text-book, the clothing fashion or the scientific theory.

Admittedly, in the area of religious faith and morals we have been rather slower to discard the old in favour of the new, for this is the aspect of human life in which conservatism has always been most strongly entrenched, for the very good reason that man looks to this area of life more than any other for his stability and security. But only small groups of religious devotees try to be consistent in their conservatism, by rigidly adhering say, to the horse and cart, sabbath observance, the castor-oil cure and the Authorized Version. The large majority of Christians have been ready to welcome the new knowledge in such things as medical science, agriculture etc., even if they have preferred to retain the orthodox religious doctrines.

This modern reversal of the relative values of the old and the new is itself quite new in man's cultural history, and that which has brought it about is the success which has attended the rise of the scientific method in the last few centuries. Our world today does not expect to find the answers to its basic questions by poring over the books of the ancient past. It looks rather to painstaking research and the assiduous application of scientific principles as the way to reach sound knowledge. We shall look briefly at some of the steps which have led to this situation, slowly at first, and in the last hundred years with breathtaking acceleration.

Perhaps Roger Bacon (1214–94) may be named as the morning-star of that adventurous questioning and experimentation which forms the basis of modern science. He was a monk, educated in the two great universities of Oxford and Paris. He undertook study and research over a wide range of subjects and is said to have spent over two thousand pounds (a large fortune in those days) on books, instruments and apparatus. He wrote that "the surest method of extirpating all heresies, and of destroying the Kingdom of Antichrist, and of establishing true religion in the hearts of men, is by perfecting a true system of natural philosophy". For this reason he freely criticized the ignorance of his fellow clerics, and went so far as to write to the Pope urging the desirability of a reformation in the church. It is not surprising that the church authorities found his presence far from comfortable, and so, for two periods totalling twenty-four years in all, he was held in close confinement in a Franciscan monastery. To appreciate the full worth of Bacon we must remember the relative ignorance which prevailed at this time. After his death his books were suppressed, though not destroyed. He is to be seen as a courageous pioneer of the attitude of free inquiry, experiment and observation.

The rise of modern science is chiefly to be seen in the Renaissance, which revived the study of the culture of ancient Greece and Rome. This in itself was an example of the ancient attitude of looking to the past for the apprehension of true knowledge, and we must freely admit that the legacy of the ancient world had a great deal to offer to fifteenth-century Europe, so much so that classical studies have remained the core of a liberal cultural education until the twentieth century.

Along with the Greek and Latin classics, the study of the Bible was revived and this contributed largely to the Reformation. It must be frankly recognized that the Bible is such a remarkable collection of books that it could more than hold its own with any set of books that had appeared up until the sixteenth century. It is not at all surprising that its rediscovery, and the acceleration of popular interest in it, made possible by the invention of printing and the growth of literacy, should have come to Europe like a fresh and powerful wind. The Bible is of such a quality that a sixteenth-century person had good reason to assume it to be thoroughly reliable upon every aspect of human existence with which it dealt.

The revival of the study of the classics of the ancient world was destined to lead to the emergence of the modern world by re-awakening that inquiring mind that marked at least some of the early Greeks. Their passion for asking questions had found no place in the dogmatic theological system into which Christianity had developed, and their concern with the natural forces of the physical world found little encouragement in a Christianity which had increasingly turned men's attention away from this tangible world, towards an unseen supernatural world.

Within two centuries, men of the calibre of Copernicus, Leonardo da Vinci, Kepler, Galileo, Gilbert, Newton and Boyle all arose to cut a path which enabled the modern world to emerge from the ancient one. Some words of Gilbert will serve to pin-point the essential new element in the pursuit of knowledge that was destined to bring increasing success. William Gilbert had a brilliant career at Cambridge in mathematics, and followed this by the study of medicine. He became personal physician to Queen Elizabeth. His most famous treatise is on the magnet, and here he sets out the experimental basis to scientific inquiry, "In the discovery of secrets and in the investigation of the hidden causes of things, clear proofs are afforded by trustworthy experiments rather than by probable guesses and opinions of ordinary professors and philosophers."

What is commonly referred to as 'modern science', heralded by Bacon in the thirteenth century, came to birth in the fifteenth and sixteenth centuries. It questioned traditional statements and beliefs and it established the experimental method. Such arguments as "the Church teaches—" were destined to become less and less sufficient to win immediate acceptance for the ideas they prefaced. The validity of traditions was questioned; general beliefs about physical phenomena were subjected to various tests.

In studying any particular field the scientist theoretically commences by accepting nothing as known with certainty. For convenience the scientific method can be set out as four basic steps, although the degree to which they can be applied in this over-simple form depends very much on the field of study. They are:

(i) the observing, measuring and gathering of all relevant data;
(ii) the ordering of the data according to whatever plan or system the data lead to most naturally, and the examination of the relationships linking them together;
(iii) the seeking of the simplest hypothesis to explain the causal relationships in the data and associated phenomena.
(iv) the testing of the hypothesis by such experiments as the data may readily lend themselves to.

With Gilbert these steps led to some remarkable results in the examination of the magnet. In the case of Galileo, the telescope was the very instrument which made experimentation possible in a way which could confirm or upset his theories of the heavenly bodies.

This method of testing traditional knowledge and of extending the content of human knowledge seems all very obvious to us today for we have become adjusted to it. We witness the marvels of technology which have been made possible through the advances of science, and we wait hopefully for the results of continuing research, for example in the cancer field. But in the sixteenth century this was a novel method of finding new knowledge. It was regarded with great suspicion, particularly when it dared to question established truth, and in the popular mind it could not be clearly distinguished from the practices of the magician, which were rightly frowned upon by the church. After all, the science of chemistry did evolve out of alchemy, i.e. the attempt to turn simple metals into gold; and the science of astronomy developed out of astrology, i.e. the attempt to read human destiny from the movement of the stars.

Only slowly did the scientific approach of questioning and testing win wider acceptance, and in doing so it set in motion the greatest revolution in human civilization that there has ever been. It was inevitable that it should lead to conflict with the conservative elements in the powerful organization of the church. Yet this conflict has often been exaggerated and misinterpreted. Bruno, it is true, lost his life in the conflict, but at a time when thousands were martyred or killed in religious wars for either the Catholic or Protestant cause, this was negligible in comparison. Nor should the conflict be interpreted as the believing church versus the non-believing scientist. The first great exponents of the emerging scientific approach were all churchmen and some of them were clerics. The conflict was between something new, pioneered by a small minority, and the *status quo*, defended by the large majority, who naturally had control of the powerful ecclesiastical machinery, and who felt themselves clearly supported by tradition, common-sense and above all divine revelation. Over the next three centuries the conservative forces at one strategic point after another were forced to surrender something which previously they had claimed to be essential to the Christian scheme of things. This conservatism had the effect eventually of causing some to abandon allegiance to the church altogether, so that then the conflict did sometimes appear to be one of the churchman versus the scientist.

The grounds on which church authorities resisted the advancing claims of the sciences were in the first place simply that they were at variance with the accepted teachings handed down from ancient times. Knowledge received from the ancient world was more likely to be true than some new-fangled notion that had not been heard of before. But the church in particular thought that its teaching possessed incontestable authority because it had been received in ancient times by divine revelation. It was confidently claimed that in the distant past, God had revealed the truth on various issues to men like Moses, the prophets, the apostles and above all through

Jesus Christ His Son, and it was therefore impossible for puny man to pit his intelligence against God, and further it was blasphemous even to question truth that was divinely revealed.

In the Middle Ages the theologians had divided the universe into two areas of experience, the natural and supernatural. While both were under the control of God, He was thought to be most distinctively known through the supernatural. At any time He chose, He could over-rule the normal processes of the natural world by His supernatural power. Not only then could God upset the experiments of the scientists, should He so choose, but also He had already delivered to the church a supernatural body of knowledge to which the experimental scientist as such had no counter.

Because the Reformation had split the Western church just prior to this time, the appeal to supernatural revelation took somewhat different forms. The Church of Rome attributed divine authority to the general corpus of Catholic teaching, which included the Bible, traditions of long standing, and the belief that the Divine Head of the church would not allow His church to err on important issues. In the Protestant churches the appeal to divine revelation was focussed on the Bible alone. By the seventeenth century this had developed into a very rigid doctrine which regarded not simply the general sense, but the very text, words, vowels and punctuation to have been supernaturally revealed by God and preserved from all error. To confound the claim of the natural scientist it was sufficient for the Catholic to hear, "The Church teaches otherwise", and for the Protestant to read in the Bible that God in His holy word had spoken differently.

But the truths being discovered by experimental science could not be silenced. They gradually grew in their power of conviction. It became necessary for Christian teachers to reduce the boldness of their claims and to readjust their thinking to the slowly emerging body of new human knowledge being brought to light by the developing sciences. This process of readjustment is still going on, and several examples will appear in the succeeding chapters. But at this point we must confine our attention to the problem that we still have to wrestle with, when we have to make a judgment between the relative merits of the knowledge inherited from the past and the new knowledge that may be gained through the developing sciences and the related fields of study, especially when these two sources appear to be in conflict with one another. In particular we must ask in what sense the church can still speak of divine revelation.

The traditional attitude which venerated the past was gradually undermined, as experimental science proved itself and opened up the door to a new world which seemed to contain unlimited possibilities. Advancing knowledge, new ideas, fresh discoveries began to accelerate the speed of change. Men were now becoming aware of change in a way that was new to them, for it was making itself evident within a man's lifetime. This has been particularly true in the nineteenth and twentieth centuries. It supplied the impetus which set the modern study of history on its feet.

As the developing sciences began to get into their stride, and that brings us into the last hundred years, there was a tendency for them, having refuted so much of what Christian orthodoxy took for granted, to establish their own form of dogmatism. The scientific hypothesis which stood repeated tests came to be regarded as the scientific law, and this soon attracted to itself an absoluteness and an authority which it was thought nothing could shake. Lesser men than the great scientists too readily assumed that all new knowledge must be made to fit the 'scientific' dogma, just as earlier it was expected to fit the ecclesiastical dogma. Indeed it has not been unknown for scientists to resist new theories on grounds which derived from the new form of dogmatism rather than those which belonged to experimental science. Something of a new cult, that has been called 'scientism', developed in the popular mind, which reflected how popular opinion had switched its allegiance from Christian orthodoxy to science and technology. The preface "The church teaches . . ." and "The Bible says . . ." came to be replaced by "Science teaches . . .", "The scientists have shown that . . ."

But dogmatism no more befits the findings of science than it does the proclamations of theology. The scientific method of study and inquiry, important and indeed essential as it is to us, does not lead us to absoluteness of truth any more than the supposed divine revelation did. All our human knowledge is subject to further correction and change, and must be adhered to with some degree of tentativeness however small. It may be likened to the frozen surface of a pond. Just because it will support a skater one day, there is no guarantee that it will do so the next. Just as fresh atmospheric conditions mean that the ice surface must first be tested afresh to see if it can be judged as safe, so our knowledge and working conclusions must be continually retested in the light of fresh data to see if we may still trust ourselves to them.

There is no source to which we can turn for knowledge which is absolute, final and unchangeable. Neither the alleged source of divine revelation, nor modern science can make this claim about the knowledge to which they lead us. What we call knowledge is our own human evaluation of what we have observed, studied, experienced, or received, and it is subject to the limitations which our own reason and language impose. We find ourselves in the paradoxical situation today where we know much more than ancient man about ourselves and our world, and yet we acknowledge we do not have the degree of certainty which often he believed he possessed. In the Middle Ages it was possible for a university man to feel himself a master of the whole body of knowledge. Today the horizons of human knowledge and inquiry are vastly extended and are still rapidly accelerating. One man can master only a tiny segment. We depend more and more upon the integrity of others for the conclusions we must accept in trust from them. Man, as a race, but not man, as an individual, is today in possession of a staggering body of reasonably reliable knowledge. Yet with all our advance, new problems have taken the place of those we have temporarily solved, new and previously unknown vistas lie beyond the peaks we have scaled, the limits of the universe seem further away than ever, and the purpose and destiny of man are not one whit clearer.

This is the situation in which we must now make some tentative judgment about the relative merits of the old and the new. Our judgment should be this—that it is false to set them over against one another as exclusive alternatives. We need both the insights of the old and the fresh truth from the new.

We must welcome the rise of the scientific method as the most valuable tool we know for the testing of existing knowledge, and for the widening of our horizon of knowledge. It has brought about a revolution in the human situation which no thinking man can ignore. Yet we must remember that the so-called laws in the natural sciences, and all knowledge derived from this new source are always subject to modification, change and replacement. The genuine scientist is always ready to question and re-test his most assured conclusions. All his knowledge is to be held with some degree of tentativeness for it is subject to reinterpretation in the light of fresh evidence.

But neither can we afford to ignore the Christian heritage which formed the basis of the European culture from which the new world and its scientific methods developed. Many things from the past may now be seen to be irrelevant, inadequate or even wrong, but not all that made the Christian heritage what it was, is false by any means and it is for this reason we are still concerned with it. Admittedly the appeal to divine revelation can no longer be made with the sure confidence that was once associated with it, for on too many occasions it has proved a faulty argument. Indeed the very term 'revelation' is today being strongly challenged as an essential term of Christian theology. In any case the Christian theologian has had to recognize that such knowledge as he may have inherited is no more absolute or final than that of the scientist. All forms of knowledge in which Christian faith and experience has expressed itself must also be continually subject to re-examination and reformulation. This is why theology at the present time is in the most fluid state it has been since the period of Christian origins.

Thus the commonly cited conflict of science versus religion, or divine revelation versus empirical science is misleading. Certainly there have been conflicts, but there have also been conflicts between different religious doctrines on the one hand and between opposing scientific theories on the other. The theologian, it is true, has had to surrender any claim to an infallible source of divine revelation, but the scientist has had to learn to resist the temptation of thinking that that is exactly what he has stumbled upon. If the word 'revelation' can still be used, then it may apply equally well to those unexpected flashes of insight received in any field of study. Theologian and scientist find that they have much more in common than is often realized. They must both be men of faith, imagination, and integrity, who are ever ready to reformulate the truths which are their chief concern in the light of that new evidence that each new day may bring. Yet they both believe that there is a constancy in the truth of man and his world that they seek to understand more clearly. The theologian describes that constancy by saying that God is the ultimate source of all truth and God is one: He is the same yesterday, today and for ever.

CHAPTER 2

The New View of the Bible

We have just seen that the theologian can no longer appeal to divine revelation with the sure confidence he once felt. While this may be conceded with regard to Christian doctrine in a general way, more yet needs to be said about the Bible, for Christians have regarded it as the focal point of revelation. If there is no special revelation, what is the origin of these 'holy' books, and how are they to be understood?

All students of theology know that in the last hundred years nothing less than a complete revolution has occurred in our understanding of the Bible. At the Reformation, and for some time later, all Christians had reasonable grounds for assuming that in the Bible they had ready access to a body of infallible knowledge which had been miraculously revealed in ancient times by direct inspiration from God. It was confidently held by both Jew and Christian that the first five books of the Old Testament had been dictated by God to Moses at Mount Sinai. It was assumed, almost without question, that the Gospel writers had faithfully delivered an accurate account of the words and deeds of Jesus.

It was inevitable that the scientific method of study should come to be applied to the Bible, and the beginnings of this were contemporaneous with the rise of experimental science. It led first to the scientific study of biblical manuscripts, known as Textual Criticism, in an attempt to establish the original text. For all the original writings have long since disappeared, and what we have left are copies of copies of copies . . . in which a large number of minor changes have occurred, mostly because of unintended mistakes when the books were copied by hand.

Once the textual critic has made the best possible reconstruction of the original Hebrew or Greek text, the biblical scholar then uses the scientific method to study the origin and content of each book of the Bible, and this was long known as Higher Criticism. He sets out to answer the following questions:

(i) What type of literature is this?
(ii) Who wrote this book?
(iii) Have any additions been made to it since?
(iv) To whom was it written?

(v) When was it written, and when were the additions made?
(vi) What did it mean to the author and his intended readers?

At the Reformation the scientific study of the Bible was in its infancy, for biblical scholars then had neither the tools nor the information adequately to examine the many traditions of authorship and date which had grown up. One of the first men to set the scientific study of the Bible on its feet was Johann David Michaelis (1717–91), a professor and prodigious scholar of Göttingen, who became a legend in his own lifetime. He wrote *Introduction to the New Testament*, in which he showed that if one accepts the ancient view that it is apostolic authorship which is the guarantee of divine inspiration, then Mark, Luke, Acts, Hebrews, James and Jude must stand on a lower level than the rest of the New Testament. It was Herbert Marsh (1757–1839), Professor of Divinity at Cambridge, who introduced the work of Michaelis into England, and who taught that Christian faith was not dependent upon a doctrine of the verbal inspiration of Holy Scripture. The then Bishop of Oxford condemned Marsh's work as "derogating from the character of the sacred books, and injurious to Christianity as fostering a spirit of scepticism".

J. G. Eichhorn (1752–1827), a student of Michaelis, has been called 'the founder of modern Old Testament criticism'. He too was a phenomenal and versatile scholar, who in 1783 completed his most famous work, *Introduction to the Old Testament*, and by 1814 had also written an *Introduction to the New Testament*. He seems to have been the first to apply systematically to the whole of the Bible the methods of Higher Criticism, a term which he himself used. From that time onwards the term 'Introduction' has been used technically to describe a book which studies the origin, authorship, date and subsequent literary history of the biblical books.

The English-speaking public first learned of what was going on, through the publication in 1860 of *Essays and Reviews* by seven Anglican scholars, six of them clergymen. One of the most debated items was an essay by Benjamin Jowett (1817–93), Master of Balliol College, Oxford, and Professor of Greek, on "The Interpretation of Scripture" in which he pleaded that the Bible should be "interpreted like any other book", maintaining that when this is done, "the Bible will still remain unlike any other book". "Any true doctrine of inspiration", he wrote, "must conform to all well-ascertained facts of history or of science." In another essay C. W. Goodwin showed that the Mosaic account of world origins could in no way be reconciled with the conclusions of science and that the popular assumption "that the Bible, bearing the stamp of

Divine authority, must be complete, perfect and unimpeachable in all its parts" could not be substantiated in the light of the host of difficulties to which it gave rise.

The book caused a great stir. A petition signed by eight thousand clergymen and addressed to the Archbishop of Canterbury asked the Bishops to take judicial proceedings against the authors. As a result, two of the contributors were suspended from office, but on appeal to the Privy Council were reinstated. The two Archbishops registered their dissent from this reversal. Then followed a renewed wave of panic. Within a few weeks eleven thousand clergymen signed a protest and one hundred and thirty-seven thousand lay-members signed an address of thanks to the Archbishops in appreciation of their recorded dissent.

In 1862 J. W. Colenso (1814–83), Bishop of Natal, published *The Pentateuch and the Book of Joshua Critically examined* in which he challenged the Mosaic authorship and the historical accuracy of these books. The storm of protest resulted in his being excommunicated and deposed from office, though he too was reinstated on appeal to the Privy Council. Such examples give an idea of the ferocity of theological debate which surrounded the revolution in Biblical studies. It continued until the turn of the century and several great scholars were deposed from their academic posts. W. Robertson Smith (1846–94) lost his chair of Old Testament studies in Aberdeen because of articles he contributed to the *Encyclopaedia Britannica*. But by the beginning of this century the new approach to the Bible had won the day in all major theological institutions of the Protestant world.

The first important result of this scientific study has been the realization that the books of the Bible were not written and published in the way a modern book is. There was no such thing as copyright, and the original author had no further control over his writing once it was out of his hand. He who legally possessed the manuscript was free to add to it or modify it if he felt led to do so. Most books of the Old Testament and some of the New Testament were not originally written in the form in which we now have them, nor was each written necessarily by one person only. In the book of Isaiah, for example, no more than about twenty chapters come from the eighth century prophet of that name, a substantial section comes from an unknown prophet of the Babylonian exile in the sixth century, some of the later chapters come from the fifth century, and a few may be as late as the fourth century B.C.

The authorship of the books has proved a very difficult problem. Scientific inquiry has shown that many of the old traditions about authorship are almost certainly false. In such cases it is usually impossible for us to learn anything definite about the identity of the real author, who in the meantime has disappeared into oblivion. We are not able to specify with confidence the author of any one of the thirty-nine books of the Old Testament, though some of the oracles of the books of the prophets originated in the mouths of the prophets there named. Luke may be the only Gospel writer whom we can actually name. There has always been a tendency to attribute stories and books to men who are already famous. It was this which caused the composite narrative of Israel's origins to be attributed to Moses, the Psalms to David, and the Epistle to the Hebrews to Paul. But though we can name fewer of the human authors of the books of the Bible than tradition thought was possible, we can on the other hand be much more definite in saying that they all had human authors. And because of this fact they reflect at many points the limited knowledge, the now outmoded conceptions, and even the personal prejudices, which were commonly held at the time of their origin.

Writing is a form of communication, and this is a process which involves two parties, a writer and his expected readers. Because there is less definiteness about the identity of the reader than there is of the author, it is a question too easily overlooked. If we are to reach an adequate understanding of the Biblical literature, the next question we must ask about each book is "To whom was it addressed?", or "For whom was it intended?" Though this sort of question cannot be answered with any great detail, as indeed it cannot be in the case of many books written today, yet even general answers are important when they deal with literature that is as old as the Bible.

The first answer that we can confidently give is that the biblical authors were writing first and foremost for the men of their own day. In some cases they were committing to writing material which already existed in oral form; in some cases they copied and adapted already existing written material; in some cases they were composing new material. But the very languages in which they wrote indicate that they were writing for men of their own time, who shared that language, and what is more important, who shared the faith which prompted them to write their own particular witness to it. There is little justification for the view held quite commonly, even if unconsciously, that the Bible consists of timeless oracles which can be equally well understood by men of all generations. Some books admittedly were of a more general character and were not tied so definitely to a particular age; one has only to note how the Psalms have been used and treasured by so many different generations. But the prophets quite definitely were addressing their fellow Israelites of their own day, and Paul was writing to particular churches about the particular problems that were besetting them.

Now if it is true that the biblical writers were writing primarily for the men of their own day, then we shall understand what they intended to communicate only by studying their words and statements within that original context to which these belong. We have all become aware of the errors we commit by quoting a verse of scripture out of context, but we have rarely appreciated how far-reaching this principle can be. To be properly understood, a verse must not only be studied in the context of the chapter and book within which it stands, but also within the social and historical context of the time when it was written, and within the personal context of the attitudes and intentions which joined the writer to his readers. The older a book is, and the more removed it is from the environment with which we are familiar, the more important this issue becomes, if we are going to deal faithfully with the words of the writer.

When the scientific study of the Bible became the storm-centre of attention in the late nineteenth century, many Christians probably consoled themselves with the thought, "It is only the Old Testament after all. We still have an absolutely reliable New Testament, and that is the essential part of the Bible for the Christian." But, of course, the New Testament was being subjected to the same kind of scientific examination. While the conclusions may not have appeared so revolutionary as with the Old Testament to begin with, they were destined to become so in the end. We now know that the Gospels were not the first New Testament books to be written, but came after Paul's Epistles. The earliest Gospel, that of Mark, was written thirty-five to forty years after the ministry and death of Jesus; those of Luke and Matthew, both of which copied sections word for word out of Mark, were written between 80 and 90 A.D.; and John's Gospel, which has quite a different style and approach, was probably written just before the turn of the century. Indeed it is likely that by the time the Gospels began to appear, not one of the original twelve disciples of Jesus was living. Actually that is probably one of the reasons why they began to appear.

These are but some examples of the problems raised and the conclusions we are led to, as soon as we ask, "When were the books of the Bible written?" Let us now turn to the question, "Why were they written?" One thing we can say with some certainty is that they were not written by their authors with any conscious intention of their being included in the Bible. On the other hand, each writer or editor did have some clear intention of his own in doing what he did, though this varied quite a bit, depending upon whether it was Amos proclaiming a divine oracle to Israel, an unknown disciple collecting his master's oracles, a priest writing down and interpreting ancient traditions, Paul writing a letter to encourage a newly founded church, or the fourth evangelist writing, as he said, "that you may believe that Jesus is the Christ, the Son of God, and that believing you may have life in his name".

Now what did the community of Israel (and later the Christian Church) believe itself to be doing in gathering together these books and eventually giving them the title of Holy Scripture? First and foremost it was setting the stamp of its authority upon what it regarded as the written record of what God had said and done through His servants in time past. Once it received this authority, the Bible became in some sense regulative for the life and faith of the community thereafter.

But the church has mostly regarded the Bible as something more than historical records, and that is why they were called *Holy* Scriptures—they had in some sense come from God. It is fairly clear what gave rise to this conviction. The Pentateuch included the record of the priestly instructions or teaching which were believed to have come directly from God through the priest, and the books of the Prophets contained the oracles which God had spoken directly to Israel through the mouth of the prophets. In the same way in the New Testament the Gospels recorded the words and acts of Jesus the Son of God.

The sense of holiness, which attached to these portions of the Bible, came to be associated with the whole, and it is only natural, as the centuries passed by, that men should come to look upon those ancient books with an increasing sense of reverence. It is further understandable that in this process the term 'Word of God', which originally could be applied quite aptly to the priestly instruction and prophetic oracle, should come to be used of the Bible, as a whole. This trend to increased veneration for the Holy Scriptures reached its peak in seventeenth century Protestantism, at which point the human origins of the Bible were almost completely overshadowed by the sense of their divine origin, and hence of their absolute infallibility at all points.

Since that time, for reasons partly mentioned above, the nature and role of the Bible has come to be seen in what is surely a more balanced perspective. This has unfortunately meant in the eyes of many that it has become for them a fallen idol. But according to the Bible itself, this is exactly what should happen to idols. That trend in the church which sought to turn the Bible into an infallible oracle was in fact a form of idolatry.

The more balanced perspective means that we accept the Bible for what it is, and that we do not try to turn it into what it is not. It means that it is not the Bible which comes under judgment, but various views, doctrines and attitudes about the Bible. The Bible cannot be changed, but the way we think about it can and must change. There is a sense in which the terms 'inerrancy', 'divine inspiration' and 'the Word of God in written form' each referred to something which is still true, but if we are going to retain these terms, we shall need to append to them so much explanation of what we mean by them, that it is better to seek fresh terms altogether. F. W. Farrar wrote in 1886, "Whoever was the first dogmatist to make the terms 'the Bible' and 'the Word of God' synonymous rendered to the cause of truth and of religion an immense disservice."

The Bible is indispensable to the Christian, for in being the only authoritative records of the origin of the faith, they become the norm for Christian faith and practice for all time. But how in practice are they to be appealed to as the norm? It is here that we must remember that both books and people are all set in a particular historical context and they cannot be properly understood in abstraction from that context. The context of the Bible is now the ancient past and the Bible is essentially a collection of voices from the past. If we are to understand these voices, we must put ourselves as far as possible into these people's historical setting and read their words through their spectacles and with their presuppositions. Having absorbed from their witness all we can, we must then interpret the substance or spirit of their witness into the context, presuppositions and thought forms of our own day.

All this means that the study and final interpretation of the Bible becomes a very skilled task. That is why Biblical scholars, theologians and ministers of the Word are necessary. The passing of time is removing us even further away from the historical context of the Bible, and so making it more difficult for the ordinary reader to have a full appreciation of what is written there. The honest reader has admitted this for a long time about many of the books of Bible, such as the prophets, the Epistles and Revelation. But while the ordinary Bible reader is increasingly dependent upon the work of the scholar, it is also true that the fruits of that scholarship are more readily available to him today than ever before.

When the aids of modern scholarship are brought to bear upon the Bible, and its own historical context is reconstructed as the stage setting, then the Bible once again becomes alive. Those

E YOU THOUGHT
OF HORTICULTURE?

SUE boat + water skier
(Peter).

WORK?
CAREER?

voices from the past speak in living, ringing tones, because for those of us whose very being has been moulded in one way or another by the Christian heritage, they are the voices of our own past who address us. To the extent that we are enabled to share with them in the crises and victories which they witnessed in their own day, the God of history, who spoke to them, then speaks His Word to us today. It is the relevant Word in the context of life which is always the Word of God that shall stand for ever.

CHAPTER 3

The New View of the World

We must now turn to that which, as much as anything else, has helped to turn the modern world into a new world. All of us have some mental picture into which we fit the particular bit of the earth's surface on which we live, and the starry sky we see at night. Although these mental pictures vary in emphasis, and in detail, and with some people they are much more hazy than they are with others, yet there are some fundamental things that they all have in common. This mental picture is the framework for what we may call our 'world view'. In the world view we share we have all been made aware of the rather insignificant role played by the planet on which we live; we know something of the solar system, and we have had impressed upon us the unbelievably immense distances which separate us from most of the stars we see in the sky with our naked eyes.

But this world view which we people of today share, regardless of our religious beliefs, is in some respects very different from that shared by the ancient world, and even from that which obtained at the Reformation. Whether we like it or not, we are separated from our fellow-Christians of the sixteenth century and earlier by virtue of a world view which causes us to think quite differently about some aspects of life on this planet. To appreciate this it is necessary to go back to the two men, who more than any others may be said to have triggered off this change in world view which has had such far-reaching implications. They are Copernicus and Galileo.

The popular view of the universe that mainly prevailed throughout the Christian era until their time, regarded the earth on which men lived as being a comparatively flat surface which stood at the very centre of the universe. Above it, in the sky, the sun, moon and stars were seen to pass over on various regular paths. Only a limited area of the flat earth and some of the sea was really known by man at firsthand, and this meant that the distant areas, either visible to his eye in the case of the sky, or surmised by him in the case of what lay under the earth, were open to a good deal of speculation, and found expression in a variety of myths.

From time immemorial the sky had been associated with the

gods, and in Christian thought this meant that the chief dwelling-place of God was the sky or heaven (in Hebrew and Greek there is only one word for both). From pre-Christian times too, man had inherited the view that the dead dwell in an underworld, that is, some supposed area below the surface of the earth, and it is fairly obvious that this notion developed from the practice of the burial of the dead. Once the doctrine of future rewards and punishments took shape, the underworld became not so much the realm of the dead as the realm of the wicked, who there suffered their deserved torment, while those destined for the blessed life with God were naturally imagined as living in the heaven or sky above.

From our own experience we can appreciate how easy it is to be content with some rather vague mental picture from which we do not attempt to draw all its logical implications. This general view varied of course in detail from age to age and from person to person. Dante and Milton bequeathed to us their epic expressions of this three-decker universe as it is commonly called today, even though Milton was living at a time when this world view was receiving the first impact of the challenge destined to destroy it.

There had been other theories of the universe put forward. About a hundred years after Christ, Ptolemy postulated that the earth was a sphere, though immovable, at the centre of the universe, round which the heavenly bodies moved. Some four hundred years earlier a Greek named Aristarchos of Samos conjectured that the sun was the centre of the universe and that the earth revolved round it. But such theories were never widely known nor did they meet with popular acceptance. Consequently, it was inevitable that the Christian faith should come to express itself within the framework of the three-decker universe just described.

The Middle Ages, particularly the twelfth and thirteenth centuries, had witnessed the revival of intellectual activity in Europe and the founding of the first universities. The philosophy and science of Aristotle (384–22 B.C.) was revived through the medium of the Arabs and the Jews, and the theology of St. Thomas Aquinas is the most famous attempt to harmonize Christian doctrine with the teaching of Aristotle. Aquinas thus established a new norm for Christian orthodoxy, and by the Reformation the world view derived largely from Aristotle had become firmly entrenched as Christian dogma and the Bible was interpreted in the light of it. They saw the universe as a series of concentric spheres surrounding the earth at their centre and in these spheres moved the planets and stars and other heavenly bodies. It was a view which seemed eminently reasonable to everyday experience.

This view of the universe was successfully challenged and

overthrown in the sixteenth century by two Christian scholars, who may be rightly regarded as laying the foundations of the modern science of astronomy. Nicolas Copernicus (1473–1543), after graduating in arts and medicine at Cracow, was professor of mathematics at Rome before he was thirty. Through the influence of his uncle, a bishop, he was invited to an ecclesiastical post at Frauenberg in his own country. It was only after he had diligently attended to his main responsibilities, such as devotional exercises and the tending of the sick, that he had spare time to devote to study and meditation. He was led to examine the earlier theories of Pythagoras (*c.* 582–500 B.C.) and Aristarchos (310–230 B.C.) which concluded that the sun and not the earth was the centre of the universe. Copernicus now revived this theory, and was able to produce some convincing arguments which seriously challenged the views of Aristotle, namely, that the earth was "fixed, immovable, and the centre of the universe".

It is now known that Copernicus reached his conclusions by about 1530, but they were not published until 1543, the year of his death, in a book entitled, *The Revolutions of the Celestial Orbs*. Copernicus knew that his conclusions were likely to meet with violent opposition from ecclesiastical authorities. Yet it was not fear which caused him to delay publication, but rather his modest and gentle nature. He was a man of deep religious faith, who did not wish to offend his fellows. He dedicated his book to Pope Paul III.

The views of Copernicus did not depart completely from the Aristotelian picture of the universe in that he still regarded the planets as moving in circular orbits round the sun. But he may be said to have put the earth in its proper place. This conclusion was soon accepted by a small and selected group of scholars in the sixteenth century and led Kepler to arrive at his exceptionally important three laws of planetary motion. But the views of Copernicus were regarded as heretical by the church authorities, and an eminent philosopher, Giordano Bruno (1548–1600), was convicted of heresy in 1594 for professing them and after six years of imprisonment in which he refused to recant, he died at the stake. He is reported to have said as he faced death, "You who sentence me are in greater fear than I who am condemned . . . this at least future ages will not deny me, be the victor who he may—that I did not fear to die. I yielded to none of my fellows in constancy and preferred a spirited death to a cowardly life."

Bruno's death was a shock to all thinking people and caused the brilliant young Italian mathematician Galileo (1564–1642) to walk with more caution. For after making some basic and shattering new discoveries about the nature of gravity, Galileo had become quite outspoken in his exposure of the falsehood embedded in Aristotelian physics and for this he quickly earned many enemies. In a letter to Kepler in 1597 Galileo confessed himself an adherent of the Copernican system but indicated that he had said nothing in public for fear that it would jeopardize his post as Professor of Mathematics at Padua.

In 1604 there blazed into the sky a brilliant new star (known to astronomers today as a nova) and Galileo, using it as an object lesson, lectured on astronomy to entranced audiences in a way which revealed his Copernican leanings. His enemies forced him into the open, and Padua became a storm-centre of controversy. Galileo was now openly committed to the new world view and the forces of the church were allied against him.

Just about this time the invention of the telescope enabled Galileo to go forward with remarkable confidence. He found mountains and craters on the moon, and this contradicted the Aristotelian belief that the face of the moon was uniformly bright. He found moving spots on the sun, which showed that the sun was rotating on its axis. He discovered four moons revolving round Jupiter, and this served as an observable model of the solar system. But not even this visible proof convinced the Aristotelians, who regarded the telescope as an instrument of deception, some refusing even to look through it at all. This latter fact has unfortunately too often characterized that conservative attitude which resolutely shuts its eyes to the new truth which disturbs the security of the *status quo*.

For some years Galileo proclaimed the new truths with great success, so much so that he was encouraged to accept a post in his native Tuscany, where his enemies were somewhat stronger. In 1615 he was summoned to Rome to explain his views to the College of Cardinals, who thereupon decided to ban the writings of Copernicus and Kepler. On the 26th February 1616, Galileo, under threat of torture, agreed 'to abandon and cease to teach his false, impious, and heretical opinions'. It has been said that no single act has done more harm to the church than Galileo's trial.

Galileo returned to his work, treading a circumspect path. He set out to write his *magnum opus*, keeping in mind the promise he had made. For this reason his book took the form of a dialogue between Salviati, a Copernican, and Simplicio, an Aristotelian. It was a brilliant piece of argument in which Salviati easily won his case. For this reason it was strange that official permission was given for its publication in 1632. The eager public reception of the book was quickly followed by ecclesiastical action, in which Galileo, now an old man, was summoned to Rome on a charge of heresy.

Remembering the fate of Bruno, and now broken in spirit, Galileo appeared before the Cardinals in penitent's garb to make a solemn act of recantation in words which were directed to be read publicly from every pulpit and within every university.

Everyone today recognizes that Copernicus and Galileo were pioneers of a view of the universe which has become universally accepted. While the church's treatment of these men is inexcusable, it is equally unfair of us from our vantage point in the twentieth century to declare how things *should* have been done. Men like Copernicus, Kepler and Galileo were producing theories which were not only not obvious, but which, in addition, seemed to be flatly contradicted by common-sense. On the other hand, the church authorities were right in being anxious to preserve the truth from being undermined by new-fangled error. The Aristotelian views by which they stood, were in their eyes not only eminently reasonable, but were thought to be inextricably bound up with the whole of Christian truth. The problem they faced was one which the church has been challenged to solve afresh at the advent of each fundamental new truth since that time. The church of Galileo's time had perhaps more grounds for feeling confidence that it was right than has been the case in subsequent dilemmas, and yet it was wrong.

The College of Cardinals believed that the Christian faith was in danger if the Copernican world view was allowed to flourish. Perhaps they sensed how far-reaching this revolution in world view could eventually be. Over the next three centuries Christians gradually became adjusted to the new ideas about space. Yet even in this twentieth century we are still feeling the repercussions of the Copernican revolution, and some of our contemporary theological debates arise from the failure to recognize what a tremendous upheaval began at that point. The Christian has withstood the full impact of the Copernican revolution for so long only by keeping his thoughts to some degree in separate compartments, namely Christian and secular. In his religious thinking he has preserved a vague mental picture of an Aristotelian kind, while in his secular thinking about space exploration he never dreams of countering the Copernican revolution.

For while from childhood we have grown up to think of the earth as a planet revolving round the sun, and are ready to try to imagine the vast stretches of space which lie beyond the solar system in all directions, when we turn our attention to most other matters of human importance, the earth's surface is for us the centre of things. Thus intellectually we see ourselves in a space-world the pattern of which was initiated for modern man by Copernicus and Galileo.

But emotionally the Biblical and pre-Copernican world views still satisfy us. This can only lead to an unhealthy, unstable, spiritual schizophrenia. This is part of the spiritual disease of the church of our day, where it fails to reconcile the new with the old.

We must briefly take note of two common methods of avoiding this schizophrenia. The first is the drastic step of abandoning the Christian faith completely as something which the modern world has shown to be quite outmoded. Some have taken this step explicitly; a much greater number have taken it implicitly, quite conscious that their remaining links with the historic roots of our culture and civilization are those of a nominal lip-service only. In some respects it is more healthy to be an honest non-Christian than a Christian schizophrenic, for the former has at least preserved some element of that integrity or wholeness of the human being for which the Christian faith expresses such concern in its Gospel of salvation.

The method of solving the problem of spiritual schizophrenia, most frequently used by professing Christians is to regard the language of the pre-Copernican world view as symbolic. All earlier affirmations about God, man and the world still stand, provided they are metaphorically interpreted. This approach is quite appealing, and contains a good measure of truth in it. But it does not go far enough, and so often in its more popular application, it does not make clear where symbol stops and reality begins. This may become clearer as we turn now to see some of the points to which the Copernican revolution leads.

We must first accept the displacement of the world from its supposed position as the immovable centre of the universe. At first sight this may appear to have little significance for the Christian Gospel. But there are far-reaching implications. It means that the earth on which we live is not the centre of the physical universe, but a comparatively small planet revolving round a very average-sized star, which in turn is but one of a hundred thousand million others forming the galaxy we call the Milky Way, and that part of the universe that our existing telescopes have so far penetrated contains about a hundred million star systems or nebulae, similar to our galaxy. Actually it is impossible for the minds of most of us really to grasp the significance of these figures, but they ought to impress upon us the almost unbelievable size of the observable universe, and the infinitesimal place in it occupied by our earth. Whether there is any organic life elsewhere in the universe, no one is able positively to affirm or deny. But the apparent lack of uniqueness of our planet makes it extremely likely that there is some kind of life elsewhere. Yet, as life has evolved on this planet to suit the complicated set of conditions that here pertain, it is unlikely that such life as may exist elsewhere will be identical with what we know or even bear close resemblance to it.

These aspects of the world in which we find ourselves today, require us to readjust our thinking about the place of man in the universe, the nature of the God who could be thought of as the Creator of this vast expanse, and the relationship, if any, which obtains between earth, man and God. The Copernican revolution has thus led us by steps to the point where God (presuming for the moment that we can still use this word in a meaningful way) must be much greater than the pre-Copernicans ever imagined, while on the other hand man, in spite of the recent rapid expanse of his knowledge and technology, appears to have been reduced to an infinitesimal role in space.

This leads us to the second and even more drastic implication. In the ancient world view the sky or heaven was regarded as the dwelling-place of God. While we cannot be sure of the extent to which the ancients interpreted this symbolically rather than literally, it can be said that some at least, if not all, thought of the divine abode in fairly materialistic terms and certainly in space terms. Heaven was a definite place in space, for it was up in the sky. Pre-Copernican man most likely accepted as fact that if by some miracle one were enabled to climb high enough in the sky, one would eventually reach the divine heaven itself. The fact that we could all laugh so knowingly when the Russian astronaut announced on his return to earth that he saw no sign of God, only shows how far we have moved since the days of Copernicus.

But it serves to accentuate the great gap that exists between our world view and that of ancient man. Our earlier Christian forebears could think of God dwelling in the upper regions, which were themselves part of the created universe. The Bible itself describes heaven as part of the universe for it affirms that God made both heaven and earth. For pre-Copernican man, heaven was itself part of the space-time continuum, that is, it was part of the created physical universe even though it was inaccessible to man. But the Copernican revolution changed man's attitude to the space which stretches out indefinitely in all directions from the earth. It has become accessible to him through the telescope and astrophysics. Man's world, which was once restricted to the inhabited surface of the earth, has now incorporated the at present immeasurable third dimension of space. Heaven, as a divine dwelling-place has disappeared from this space-time continuum. If the word heaven is still to convey some meaningful content, then it must be interpreted in terms different from those of space.

But in turn the disappearance of the divine abode from the space universe has far-reaching implications for those foundation affirmations of the Christian Gospel known as the Resurrection and Ascension of Jesus Christ. From the end of the first century onwards the proclamation of the Christ risen and ascended came to be understood in something like the following terms: on Easter Day the crucified body of Jesus was restored to life by God, and came forth from the tomb, and appeared to men. The body of the risen Lord may not have been wholly identical with the pre-crucifixion body, for it could appear and disappear, and pass through closed doors. But it was so related to the previous body, that none of the latter remained in the tomb, for it was empty, and, according to certain reports, the risen Christ ate and drank with his disciples just as he had before his death. After appearing to them for a period of forty days, this risen Jesus ascended to the dwelling-place of God in the heavens above, there to sit at the right hand of God. Christians hopefully looked to the day when from that same heaven this Jesus would descend in all his glory and establish his permanent Kingdom on earth.

Now this version of the Resurrection and Ascension excited awe and wonder in the minds and hearts of those who heard it, but at least it was meaningful and even to a certain degree reasonable within the ancient world view. The idea of a physical body from this earth being raised to the heavenly sphere above did not appear impossible, even if it rarely happened. The Old Testament told stories of how Enoch and Elijah had made similar ascensions. But the disappearance of this kind of heaven from our space universe according to our contemporary world view removes this version of the Resurrection and the Ascension from the miraculous to the meaningless. It is interesting to note that the need for reinterpretation of these foundation affirmations first showed itself to be necessary in the account of the Ascension, for it was at this point that the implications of our world view first became obvious. Only later was it recognized that one cannot consistently offer some kind of spiritual interpretation to the Ascension and at the same time think of the Resurrection in physical terms.

Of course many attempts have been made to reconcile the traditional account of the Resurrection and Ascension to our world view, but no amount of manipulation of detail will really achieve this. The three-decker world view of ancient man, and the contemporary space universe which stems from Copernicus and Galileo are so different from each other, that every aspect of the Christian faith on which cosmology impinges must be radically reinterpreted.

There is no indication that these particular implications of the Copernican revolution were foreseen in the seventeenth century, or the opposition of ecclesiastical authority may have been even more violent. Even today, some three hundred years later, devout Christians find some of them hard to adjust to. The College of Cardinals refuted the views of Copernicus on what appeared then to be very sound reasoning. They were the guardians of the body of Christian teaching, and this incorporated knowledge which, as they thought, had been communicated to man by God Himself, and consequently all future discoveries by man were bound to conform to the truth already received. We have seen that this view of divine revelation has had to be surrendered; it was the new world view among other things, which made this necessary and perhaps, as yet, we are only at the beginning of all the implications of the new space world to which Copernicus and Galileo introduced us.

CHAPTER 4

The New View of Origins

At the beginning of the modern era all Europeans, whether Catholic or Protestant, shared a common view of the origin of the world in general and of man in particular. This common view came from the opening chapters of the Bible. No cogent evidence had so far been produced to cause any widespread questioning of these chapters, and since they had long been regarded by the church as divinely delivered to Moses, this account of origins was accepted as sufficient and final.

The common view was that God created the whole universe out of nothing, about six thousand years ago (a notable Irish theologian, James Ussher (1581–1656), deduced from the chronology of the Bible that the actual year was 4004 B.C.) It all happened in the remarkably short period of six days, and on the sixth day God made both the animals and human beings. First of all from the dust of the ground He made one human being; He breathed His own spirit into him and called him Adam. Then from Adam's rib He fashioned a woman called Eve. All other human beings were subsequently descended from these two by natural procreation.

It was further believed that the human race became so evil that God almost annihilated them by a great flood that covered the earth. Consequently all men who lived after the flood down to the present day have been the descendants of Noah, who became with his family the sole human survivors of the Deluge. The nations of the world were thought to have spread over the earth subsequent to that time and to have developed gradually their racial characteristics, their separate languages having resulted from a further divine judgment, following the disastrous attempt to build the Tower of Babel. All human religion, other than the Judeo-Christian faith was thought to consist of various forms of natural religion which could all be traced back to Noah. This simple outline in the opening chapters of Genesis was thought to contain all that man could ever know of the origin of the earth and of the human race. All Christians and Jews, and that meant nearly all Europeans, accepted this simple view of origins as a matter of course until about a hundred years ago, and some Christians still cling firmly to it with varying modifications.

The nineteenth century was destined to witness the complete upset of this simple picture, and this upheaval began with the emerging science of geology. In his book, *Principles of Geology*, 1830, Charles Lyell (1797–1875) burst through the preconceived opinions that had hindered earlier geologists, and from the evidence he had amassed he showed that the earth had been in existence for a far greater period than the Bible allowed for. Where men had thought in thousands of years, he claimed that 'the language of nature signified millions'. He explained the present condition of the earth's surface as the result of gradual development over a long period and due to causes which were still at work. He claimed on the evidence of fossils that life had existed on the earth for millions of years. Ardent defenders of the Bible refused to accept these conclusions, and one of them, a zoologist named P. H. Gosse (1810–88) admitted all the evidence of geology but claimed that at the creation God had deliberately placed the fossils in the rock so that men would later find them there. In the same way he concluded that Adam and Eve had navels just as if they had been born naturally as infants. Bertrand Russell later commented that on this theory we might all have come into existence five minutes ago, with ready-made memories, holes in our socks and hair that needed cutting.

But the problem posed by the much longer history of the earth was small compared with the furore which took place soon after the publication in 1859 of the *The Origin of Species* by Charles Darwin (1809–82). (We should note that this was two years prior to the famous *Essays and Reviews*.) Darwin originally went up to Cambridge to study for Holy Orders, but he became absorbed in natural science. After some thirty years of study, including several trips of exploration round the world, Darwin outlined a theory of biological evolution, which was destined to revolutionize the common view of the origins of life. The idea of evolution was by no means new and Darwin's own grandfather was a zealous exponent of some form of evolution or development. It was Darwin's achievement to supply the theory with a tenable principle, namely, that progressive changes take place by a process of natural selection.

One can readily see that the theory of biological evolution is completely at variance with what had hitherto been the common view of origins. Instead of tracing man's ancestors back to our first two parents, Adam and Eve, it explains man's origins as all a part of a very long and very intricate process of development, in which all known species of life had by natural selection gradually branched out from other forms; this tree of life had grown originally from the simplest possible forms of life. What had previously appeared simple and straightforward was now bristling with new problems. In the old view all the ancestors of present-day man had been true men, but in the evolutionary picture man's original ancestors were not men at all, and it became impossible to point to a time when true men first appeared and why. The orthodox Christian teaching about the creation of man and the origin of sin in a first act of disobedience in Eden now appeared to be undermined. Such problems as these were more difficult to solve than the fact that the opening chapters of Genesis could no longer be regarded as history and needed to be reinterpreted.

In view of the difficulties raised for Christian orthodoxy by the theory of evolution it is the more remarkable to find that there were theologians who reacted favourably to Darwin's book from the very beginning. F. J. Hort (1828–92) one of the famous trio of Cambridge Biblical scholars of last century, himself skilled in both classics and natural science, wrote in a private letter in March 1860, "Have you read Darwin? . . . In spite of difficulties I am inclined to think it unanswerable." Cardinal Newman (1801–90) wrote in a private note-book in 1863, "It is strange that monkeys should be so like men with no historical connection between them. I will go the whole hog with Darwin, or dispensing with time and history altogether, hold not only the theory of distinct species, but also of the creation of fossil-bearing rocks."

It is a pity that these initial thoughts of men like Hort and Newman were not made public till long afterwards. For in these words Newman expressed succinctly the dilemma in which the Christian was placed; he had either to shut his mind completely to the new knowledge derived from science, or he had to be prepared to accept it and surrender the security and some of the claims of traditional orthodoxy. Charles Kingsley (1819–75), a clergyman whose theological competence has been obscured by his literary fame, was ready to accept the voice of science as the voice of God, and believed that the theologian was bound to be obedient to it. He maintained that all ordinands should be required to study at least one of the sciences.

But in the decade following the publication of *The Origin of Species* it was mainly the voices of reaction that were heard. The book gave rise to a famous debate between Samuel Wilberforce (1805–73), Bishop of Oxford and T. H. Huxley (1825–95) the celebrated biologist. The Bishop made a vigorous, polished but superficial speech attacking Darwin's theory and concluded by trying to win the sympathy of the audience with an appeal to Victorian sentimentality concerning women. "If anyone were to be willing to trace his descent through an ape as his grandfather", he asked, "would he be willing to trace his descent similarly on the side of his grandmother?" It is reported that Huxley excitedly murmured to his neighbour, "The Lord hath delivered him into mine hands," an odd remark to come from the first man to call himself an agnostic. Huxley then gave a straightforward account of Darwin's views and ended by declaring that he would rather have a monkey for a grandfather than one who used his great gifts to stifle truth.

Even Wilberforce, however, was ready to recognize some cogency in evolution and this is borne out by the way he reviewed *The Origin of Species* later that same year. There he accepted the principle of natural selection but argued that it could not by itself account for man's moral and spiritual condition. He defined his attitude towards scientific truth in the following striking way, "We have no sympathy with those who object to any facts in nature . . . because they believe them to contradict what it appears to them is taught in Revelation . . . To oppose facts in the natural world because they seem to oppose Revelation . . . is . . . but another form of lying for God, and trying by fraud or falsehood to do the work of the God of truth . . . The words graven on the everlasting rocks are the words of God and they are graven by His hand." He claimed that these could not 'contradict His word written in His book'.

Only two of the famous *Essays and Reviews* touched upon *The Origin of Species*. We have already referred to the one by Benjamin Jowett; the other was written by an accomplished scientist and Professor of Geometry at Oxford, Baden Powell. (His name is familiar because of his son—the founder of the Boy Scout Movement.) Baden Powell believed that it was within the power of science to make rapid advances in human knowledge in all directions and to unravel sooner or later those mysteries which at the moment seemed miraculous and mysterious. Such a contention was a great blow to orthodox theology for the most popular method in those days of defending the truth of the Christian faith was to appeal to prophecy and the record of the miracles. If the concept of miracle were to vanish, as a mirage, before the advance of science, what was to happen to Christian apologetics?

Baden Powell accepted biological evolution enthusiastically, writing, "a work has now appeared by a naturalist of the most acknowledged authority, Mr. Darwin's masterly volume on the Origin of Species by the law of 'natural selection', which now substantiates on undeniable grounds the very principle so long denounced by the first naturalists . . . a work which must soon bring about an entire revolution of opinion in favour of the grand principle of the self-evolving powers of nature." The latter was a prophecy soon to be fulfilled.

There were many, of course, who were quite unprepared for this revolution in the understanding of the origins of life. One clergyman is said to have prayed in church, "O Lord, grant this evolution be not true, but if it is, grant that it may be hushed up as far as possible." It is not surprising that the advent of Darwin's theory of evolution should have caused such consternation in Christian circles, for it removed what appeared to many to be an indispensable pillar of the whole building of Christian orthodoxy. Among more conservative Christians that reaction has continued up until the present, and where such conservatism has been the dominant force in society, it has even been forbidden to teach biological evolution in the schools.

More than once in Christian history Christians have concluded too quickly that if a particular doctrine is proved false, then the whole Christian faith becomes null and void. Such an unthinking zeal to defend the faith can have an effect just the opposite of that desired. When Christians claim that a particular doctrine must be defended at all costs or else Christianity is doomed, those who cannot accept the particular doctrine can hardly be blamed if they assume this must be so, and, as a consequence, surrender with reluctance all allegiance to the Christian faith. T. H. Huxley and Charles Darwin themselves were by no means antagonistic to the Christian faith; it was the unwillingness of Christians to face new truth which forced men of this calibre further away from the faith than they themselves would have chosen to go. T. H. Huxley, in spite of his outspoken criticism of orthodoxy and of the church, was still at the end of his life advocating that the Bible be taught in schools in order to foster sound morality and a religious sense. The theory of evolution, and the church's failure to appreciate it, became one of several factors, which have helped to bring about that decline in active Christian allegiance which has so marked the last hundred years.

For though Darwin's particular theory of biological evolution was destined to undergo changes and modifications in the hands of successive biologists and zoologists (and with this we are not here concerned), there can be no going back to the simple Biblical picture of origins which was commonly held before Darwin. This picture has been shattered once and for all. Biological evolution is not only universally accepted by all scientists in some form or other, but it is part of the common knowledge of nearly everybody who has had a secondary school education. All this has taken place in the last hundred years, and the popular spread of this view in the last thirty or forty years.

The new idea of origins is much vaster and more complicated than the Biblical one it has replaced. At a conservative estimate the story of man's origins takes us back at least half a million years and man has been civilized for only about two per cent of this period. The evidence suggests that in the long process of evolution several types of man emerged, but only our own species, *Homo sapiens*, has survived. The period of time which witnessed the divergence of these hominoid or human species from the various species of anthropoid apes may take us back from ten to twenty-five million years. Most of us have little real appreciation of what a vast time span this represents, and it raises many fascinating questions for which, as yet, there are no clear answers. For such knowledge as we do have, we are dependent upon anthropology.

Yet the period which has witnessed the development of men, long as it may appear to us, is short when compared with the vaster period over which other forms of life appeared. To trace the emergence of mammals we must go back two hundred million years, and for the origin of the earliest forms of life we go back three thousand million years. Much of the rapid and important achievement in the fields of zoology, botany and biochemistry, is too technical for the average layman readily to appreciate. Sufficient it is to say that the story of the earth with the various forms of life that have come to appear on it, is a million times longer than people of only a century ago used to think it to be.

But when we look out from the earth to seek to understand the universe of which our planet is such an infinitesimal part, and to ask how it all began, we find ourselves in a bewilderingly vast space which just defies our imagination. Even though we may read about it from time to time, very few of us live our lives in conscious awareness of this space universe. Mostly we are caught up with what is going on in our own little neck of the woods, and are not even aware of the diversity of the human situation scattered over the face of the globe, let alone the staggering immensity of the universe. Yet if we are going to live in the real world, we must try to understand to some degree the universe that astronomy and astrophysics have opened to us. It is so large that quite a different unit of measurement has to be used—the lightyear. But to say that a certain star is so many hundreds of lightyears away does not really mean much to minds which are accustomed only to the inch or the mile, which can be roughly measured with the eye.

How old is the universe? Did it have a beginning at all, or has it always existed in one form or another? In any case, is there anything but a theoretical difference between a billion billion years and eternity? Did the universe begin with a 'big bang', as has been suggested, or is it subject to a process of continuous creation? With such questions as these we have no assured results at all as yet. Astronomy and radio-physics are amassing more and more information about the universe, and they may eventually be able to give us more definite answers. But here is the point. We once thought we had the answers and they seemed relatively simple and straightforward. Now the whole picture of the universe and the question of its origins have become tantalizingly out of reach of the minds of most of us.

In this greatly changed world of space and time, what does it mean to say that the God, who supposedly cares for us like a father, is also Creator? How can we call Him Creator, if it turns out there has never been a time when the universe did not exist in one form or another? Is man the peak of all creation, or only of those forms of life that have evolved on this one tiny planet? If man has evolved out of lower forms of life, at what point did he become man, and what is it that constituted true humanity? And if there was no point in time when man first fell into sin, what does it mean to speak of man in his fallen state, and how did sin, if this is still the proper term, come to enter the human scene? These are some of the questions which the new view of origins has raised for the Christian, and which must receive a satisfactory answer if the Christian faith is to survive as a living force in the new world. For though there is more to be learned about origins, which may do much to fill in the great gaps in our knowledge, and which may necessitate further radical revision in understanding, one thing is certain, and that is that the popular and simple view of origins which obtained among Christians until a hundred years ago has gone for ever.

CHAPTER 5

The New View of Man

From within this new view of the world and its origins, we must now discuss the nature of man himself, as we have been led to understand him by all those sciences most closely related to him, such as anthropology, anatomy, physiology, neurology, psychology and sociology.

It has long been recognized that man has so much in common with the animals that he must be regarded as an animal, even if of a very special kind. The Bible itself placed men and animals in the same category by describing their creation on the same day and thus distinguishing them as a class from all other created forms of life. In 1555 an early French zoologist, called Belon, showed from the comparison of the skeletons of a bird and a man that there was such a remarkable similarity, that man carried about in his own body the proof of his connection with the animals.

But man has also drawn a clear line of distinction between himself and all other animals, and in traditional Christian teaching this was done by stating that man consisted of two parts—a body and a soul. It was the body which linked him with the animals; it was made of similar flesh and bone, and lived only for the limited period between birth and death, at which point the body fell into decay. That which made man unique was the possession of a soul, which, being spiritual and not material, was thought to survive the death of the body and go to live in a spiritual realm. The soul, involving the consciousness, the memory and the essential self, was thought capable of existing as a complete living entity apart from the body.

At a time when men knew very little about the functioning of the human body, this view seemed to be largely a matter of commonsense. The soul was what he knew in his own inner experience of thought, feelings and acts of decision. (In his dreams, just as real to ancient man as waking impressions, his soul often seemed to leave the sleeping body and visit far places.) Without even thinking about it, he projected this same spiritual entity into the creatures round about him. For very ancient man, the whole world was alive with the kind of life he knew within himself. Rivers, trees, mountains, birds, animals all possessed their particular kind of spirit or soul. This early attempt to explain the real world is called animism and it has been almost universal at a particular stage in man's cultural development.

It was quite a step forward when men first began to distinguish inanimate objects, such as stones, from animate or living creatures. It was a further step forward when the uniqueness of man was recognized. This was not nearly as obvious as it may appear to us. In some societies the line of division was not drawn so clearly between men and the animals, as between the nobility and the peasantry, the latter being treated with much the same attitude as the animals. Even up till modern times class and caste divisions have obscured the unity of the human species, while animal lovers have frequently projected their own human consciousness into animal experience.

It further seemed a matter of common-sense to ancient man that this inner spirit or soul, which he knew from the inside and which he witnessed in his fellows, should be immortal or deathless. On the negative side, no living person had any subjective experience of death, and on the positive side, the dead person who appeared and spoke to him in his dreams seemed just as alive as ever. Indeed it is much easier to imagine the souls of the dead living on in some new kind of existence than it is to accept as fact that they have really died. Even in our own experience today we find it hard to realize completely what death means when it occurs to someone with whom we have lived closely. It is much easier to assume they are still alive but somewhere out of our sight. Archaeology has shown that from the beginnings of civilization man has evidently believed in the continuance of the soul after death, and has buried his dead in such a way as to provide for them the things thought necessary for the next life.

The speculation which accompanied the belief in a deathless human soul took different forms in different cultures. In India, for example, it took the form of a transmigration of souls, or reincarnation. The soul was regarded as an indestructible entity, which had neither beginning nor end, but which migrated from one body to the next, without any way of escaping from the endless procession. The souls of gods, devils, men, animals and insects were all of the same order, and so the kind of creature into which one's soul would be reborn depended on the kind of life one lived. The soul did not carry over any memory, but it did retain traits, skills etc. The various gospels of salvation provided by Hinduism and Buddhism sought to rescue the soul from its endless wandering and attendant suffering.

The belief that man possesses a soul, or some kind of spiritual entity that survives death, is itself an almost universal phenomenon in primitive human culture and it has led to different kinds of development in maturer human civilizations. It was this primitive understanding of the nature of man which was given clear and classical exposition in the writings of the Greek philosopher Plato (427–347 B.C.) He saw the soul as the source of movement in every body which moved of itself, and because the soul is thus self-moving, it must be unbegotten and immortal. For Plato, God is the Supreme Soul and all living creatures have souls created by God and these are the source of everything good and bad. When the body of a man dies, then the soul is released, as from a prison, for fuller life in a spiritual realm.

It is nowadays widely recognized that what became the orthodox Christian doctrine of the soul owes more to Platonic philosophy than to any other source. This may come as a surprise to those who have assumed that Christian doctrine has always drawn its substance from the Bible. It must be remembered that the early Christian community moved almost wholly into the Gentile world within a generation or two after its origin within Judaism, and that, as Christian thought took more definite shape within the next three or four centuries, it was inevitable that it should have been strongly influenced by the prevailing philosophy of the Hellenistic culture in which the church moved. This is strikingly illustrated by the fact that when the Renaissance initiated a revival of Platonism, some Christian scholars, known as the Cambridge Platonists, urged the return of Christian theology to 'its old loving nurse, the Platonic philosophy'.

While Christian doctrine was still passing through its formative period, Christian scholars such as Clement of Alexandria (*c.* A.D. 150–215), Origen (*c.* A.D. 185–254), Augustine (A.D. 354–430), the last being the most influential of all in Western Christianity, were strongly influenced by Platonism in their formulation of the Catholic doctrine of the soul. For them the soul could be understood, in clear contrast to the body, as the essential spiritual man; the soul included the seat of consciousness, it was the storehouse of knowledge and hence included the human memory, it was the cause of goodness and evil, and it was deathless or immortal. Although such a doctrine of an immortal soul is usually appealed to in order to answer questions about the meaning of death, it is logical to assert that the soul, whose existence is independent of the body, may therefore originate independently from the body. Christian speculation was sometimes led to debate whether God created the particular human soul at the time of conception, or whether the soul had a pre-existence which preceded the mortal life for which it was destined. Charles Lamb gives us a moving portrayal of pre-existence in his essay "Dream Children".

It is possible to trace the popular view of man, as the temporary combination of a mortal body and an immortal soul, back through Christian orthodoxy to Platonism and from there to primitive animism. It may have been noticed that so far the Biblical view has not been mentioned. Now it is true that certain Biblical passages were used to support this view, but this was largely because the doctrine was read into them, an easy temptation to fall into at any time. Modern Biblical scholarship has been able to show that this view of man is almost wholly foreign to the Old Testament and plays very little part in the New Testament. More will be said on the Biblical view of man later, but it is sufficient to point out here, that it is just because the Bible hardly anywhere reflects a doctrine of an immortal soul, that the Christian hope took the form of the resurrection of the body.

But in the modern world several sciences have converged to press home to us the rational conclusion that each individual man is a psychosomatic unity, a living physical organism whose various organs, both physical and psychical, can only function as part of the total organism. There are certain minor parts of the body which man can lose and yet still live and be truly man, such as hair, teeth, appendix and even limbs. But there are major organs, the loss of any one of which brings death to the whole organism.

Now words like 'mind', 'will', 'spirit' and 'soul' are abstractions, which we have found useful in order to describe the highest levels of human existence as they are understood by our thinking powers, and experienced in that most mysterious element of all—our stream of consciousness. But what we are trying to describe, by each of these abstract terms, is essentially dependent for its reality upon the continuous functioning of the total organism, with all its essential physical organs and biochemical processes. Thus, just as the loss of an essential organ brings the death of the whole organism, so the death of the physical organism brings to an end those psychical or spiritual aspects of a man which are usually thought of as characterizing his uniqueness.

The whole animistic approach to man, which in both religious thought and philosophical analysis can be traced back to man's earliest attempts to understand himself, has been destroyed by the modern sciences most closely related to the study of man. Now it must be confessed that this is a conclusion reached almost wholly on rationalistic, and, some would say, materialistic grounds. It is for this reason that it may be argued that these sciences have not exhausted all that is to be said about man, or even touched the most important questions about human existence. This we may readily concede, and many neurologists, psychologists, biochemists etc., would willingly agree; but no understanding of man can be any longer satisfactory, which is content to ignore what these sciences have taught us about the nature of man as a psychosomatic organism.

Whereas pre-scientific man had only vague notions of how the mind, spirit and consciousness of man were related to the body, we now have sufficient knowledge of the brain and the nervous system to know that man's stream of consciousness could not function at all if it were not regularly receiving sense impressions from the eye, the ear, and touch etc. The human consciousness is dependent for its vitality, interest and development on keeping open at least some of these channels, which are the only means of contact man has with the world around him. Such controlled experiments, as it has been possible to conduct in order to learn what happens when a man is deprived of all his senses, suggest that the mind is soon subject to increasing hallucination, such as could quickly lead to the loss of the rational stream of consciousness so essential for true humanity. Thus man cannot be abstracted completely from his environment without soon ceasing to be human.

We know too that the memory, without which man could have no sense of continuity, is dependent upon the storage capacity of the unbelievably large number of brain cells, so that to the lay mind the brain is as close to an electronic computer as anything could be. We have learned how physical damage to the brain impairs the functioning of various parts of the body to which the nervous system connects it, and severe brain damage of a congenital nature can prevent the development of anything like a genuinely human personality altogether. Severe brain damage due to accident in later life, on the other hand, can make such radical changes in the personality, or destroy so much of the personality as to make it impossible to say whether it is the same person any more, even though it is fundamentally the same physical body.

In the light of this essential interdependence of mind and brain, spirit and body, we come to see that a disembodied soul is not only an unsatisfying state of existence to contemplate, but it is also bereft of any real meaning. What kind of existence can a soul have which can receive no sense impressions and make no physical response, and hence have no communication and no communion with other souls? What kind of a soul can it be that has no memory? The ancients, too, vaguely sensed these difficulties, and always imagined the spirit or soul as having some body or form, even though, of necessity, it had to be of a ghostly or ethereal 'substance', and pictured a spirit or soul world in which the soul found community

Depth psychology and psychiatry have approached the understanding of man's mind and soul (psyche) from an angle rather different from that of neurology and biochemistry. Instead of trying to penetrate to the mind and will by physical methods, they seek to understand the individual man through the channel of speech communication which constitutes one's only means of access to what, for convenience, we call the mind. Psycho-analysis has brought to light the fact that the stream of consciousness of which each person is aware in his inner self is but the highest level of the complicated processes which are at work in the psyche. Below the conscious stream there is a great mysterious area, now called the subconscious, where, at differing levels, there move emotional forces set in operation by past experiences. It may be likened to that large part of every iceberg which lies hidden below the surface of the water. We now know that much of the emotions we feel, the thoughts we pursue, and the decisions we make, have at least been influenced, and sometimes largely directed, by those forces of which the subject himself is not consciously aware. Thus each individual is a far more complicated being than he realizes, and his own conscious assessment of himself, his motives, his emotions and his desires is only a rough over-simplification, and very likely a distorted one at that.

When the psychologist turns his attention to the study of religious behaviour, he can often give a new and quite different explanation for such experiences as dramatic conversions, visions or the sense of being impelled by a supernatural force from without. Whereas the religious believer has interpreted these as due to the influence of the Spirit of God, the psychologist is aware of the many emotional tensions at work in the human mind, only some of which are realized by the subject himself. For example, it is an observable fact that it is in those churches where dramatic conversions during adolescence are highly rated and are expected, that they actually occur in significant numbers. The psychologist interprets this as due to the fact that the adolescent is unconsciously under the pressure to do that which his particular community expects of him.

This leads us to see how sociology is bringing home to us the fact that a man must not be thought of as a self-contained unit in isolation from his social setting. Such a view is an unreal abstraction. Man is essentially a social creature, and it is due in no small measure to this, that human civilization has evolved, and man has reached the point where he is today. Each generation emerges out of the preceding one. Each man is a child of his generation, and of his immediate social setting. His family life, his school, his clubs and his whole cultural background have contributed to make him what he is. That is why we now recognize that the man with criminal tendencies is not always wholly to blame. He too reflects his upbringing, his environment and the tensions in his society. For the same reason the religious beliefs and allegiance of a man are nearly always those of his own family, or of his immediate cultural setting. In his own experience he may have consciously adopted them and made them his own, but because man is so dependent on the cultural influences around him, this was already largely predetermined.

Whereas sociology studies the nature of society and the interplay between the individual and society, education studies the learning ability of man at various stages and tries to find those teaching methods which will be most fruitful in leading the individual to full maturity within his society. As an infant, the human creature is more helpless and dependent than most other creatures. It is this initial helplessness which gives him the freedom to learn most from his social environment. The period of his greatest readiness to learn coincides with the period in which his body and physiological functions are growing to maturity. Some time thereafter the learning ability usually tapers off, though it may vary considerably from person to person. Patterns of thought and behaviour grow more rigid, and it becomes increasingly unlikely, though never impossible, that the person will abandon those patterns for new ones. This leads to two relevant observations about the nature of man. The religious beliefs and attitudes, with which a man will go through life, will be largely those which he has been led to embrace during the first twenty-five years. In later life he will not be as free as we often think him to be to make a favourable response to the claims of Christian allegiance. On the other hand, in the case of a person who has embraced certain Christian beliefs and attitudes in his formative years, his continued manifestation of these in later years may be due not simply to strength of conviction, but to the fact that they have become so much a part of him, that it would require a very strong challenge to cause him to abandon them.

All these studies bring home to us as never before the creatureliness and earthliness of man. Man himself is all a part of the natural world. As with all forms of life on this planet, man as an individual has a beginning at birth, he grows to maturity, he proceeds to a period of flowering, and then, if his life has not been terminated prematurely, he experiences a period of slowing down in both his physical and mental powers before these signs of wear and decay finally lead up to his death. While man is a many-sided and most complex creature, he is essentially a unity in whom the physical and psychical so penetrate one another as to be necessarily interdependent. When man dies, it is the whole psychosomatic organism which dies. Man, like all other forms of terrestrial life from which he has evolved, is a physical mortal creature, whose life is lived within those limits of space and time to which his creatureliness subjects him.

It is not that this view of man is wholly new. Aspects of it have forced themselves on man's attention from time to time, at least as far back as we can trace his thoughts. But because man has risen to the spiritual level where he has become aware of his creatureliness and knows he must die (and so far as we know he is unique in this respect), he has also rebelled against this prospect and sought to escape from it. The chief avenue of escape he found was by way of that animism which led in turn to a belief in the immortality of the human soul.

It hardly needs to be said that the new view of man, to which today's studies and sciences are leading us, constitutes a severe challenge to the doctrine of man assumed and taught by Christian orthodoxy. For one thing, man's free-will is a good deal more limited than is often supposed, and a few people have even been led to the conclusion that it is an illusion. While there are still good reasons for believing that man *does* have some freedom of choice at his highest level of consciousness, it is a freedom within a context of very severe limits, which have been imposed upon him by his creatureliness. The kind of person he is, the values he acknowledges, the beliefs he holds, have been to quite a large extent determined by forces over which he has had no control. They constitute a tremendous complex of instincts and inherited traits, family and cultural background, education, and all the aspects of the individual's own past experience which remain in his memory and in his unconscious as continuing motivating forces.

The dogmatic way in which the church has often declared itself on matters of personal salvation and judgment has rested on an inadequate understanding of the complexities of the human situation. Further, the challenge of the new view of man to the traditional form of the Christian answer to the question of his ultimate destiny is almost as devastating as it could be. It is not at all surprising that in the last two or three generations this answer has been regarded in the lands of Christian culture with rapidly diminishing conviction. Not only has there been a complete collapse of the world view of heaven, earth and hell, in which the answers concerning human destiny were expressed, but the very nature of man, as two separable parts of body and soul, which Christian orthodoxy has long taken for granted, can no longer be reconciled with our present knowledge of man.

Let it be said here and now, however, that we need not conclude that the very sciences which are forcing us more and more to abandon as invalid our traditional understanding of the nature and destiny of man, have thereby solved the riddle of life and of the mystery of man. Far from it! They have shown up that problem in stark relief. The enigma of human existence has become a greater mystery than ever. They have shown us that the form in which man's eternal hope was expressed is no longer a satisfying one, and that any fresh expression of this hope must take fully into account all that we have learned about our creatureliness and our mortality. But because man cannot live for long in a context which has for him neither meaning nor hope, a fresh and satisfying expression of the answers to these basic questions has become a matter of extreme urgency for the future of mankind.

CHAPTER 6

The New Secular Culture

How has the life of our world today already reacted to, and to a large extent been moulded by, the new views of man and his world that we have just been considering? The word which best describes the dominant trend in our world today is secularization. By this word it is commonly implied that more and more of man's life is being emancipated from the concern of religion, and hence from the power of church authorities. One area after another, such as healing, education and politics, has been secularized. In view of this it is not surprising that Christians have most commonly been led to regard secularization as an enemy to be fought. In their eyes it is the modern manifestation of the earlier foes of Christianity, such as paganism and apostasy. The church often sees itself as an army engaged in an orderly retreat to defensive positions from which, when the time is ripe, it will sally forth to win back to true religious faith those areas of human life, which for the moment are in the hands of the secularist forces.

Although most of the present activity of the church seems to rest on such a view as this, we do well to ask whether this is not altogether too superficial a diagnosis of our present situation. We must not hide our eyes from the fact that what we have called secularization is an entirely new phenomenon in human history, that it has been brought about by a number of new factors in human knowledge, the more important of which we have looked at, and that for these reasons a secularized culture has come to stay, at least in some form. Certainly there will be changes in the future which we cannot now foresee, but it is unreasonable to suppose it at all likely that there will be a return to the pre-secular world. To appreciate this contention, we must examine secularization a little more closely.

We can learn something first of all from the very curious history of the word 'secular'. It is derived from the Latin word *saeculum* which meant a long period of time, and in particular the age or period of world history to which the present belongs. One age or *saeculum* when it comes to an end was thought to be followed by another, which could, of course, be very different in character. Endless time was described in the phrase *in saecula saeculorum*, translated 'for ever and ever'. It is worthwhile mentioning that the equivalent Greek word *aeon*, along with its derivatives, occurs quite often in the New Testament and is translated as 'eternity', and 'eternal'.

Now the word *saeculum* came to mean 'the world of this present age', i.e. the present world. In Christian usage in the course of time we find the word 'secular' being used to describe this visible tangible world in contrast with another world, the unseen supernatural world, which is the world of eternity. Any activity directed mainly to the natural world is described as secular, while any activity directed to the supernatural world is 'religious'. The distinction was found in the Christian priesthood. Those who withdrew from the world to live the life of Christian devotion in the monastic cloister were the 'religious', while those who ministered in the everyday world were the 'secular' priests.

Medieval Christendom was subject to a dualistic tension between the secular and the religious, the temporal and the eternal, which made itself evident at many points. Society itself closely reflected the commonly accepted Christian view of the individual man as a combination of a visible body and an invisible soul. The state or kingdom was the 'body' of society and was ruled by the secular prince or king; the church was the 'soul' of society and was ruled by the prince of the church. As practically all Europeans were Christians, the powers of church and state were geographically co-terminous. The interests of the two powers penetrated each other at all points, and this led to conflict, of a kind that a man may feel in his own experience when the flesh and the spirit are at war. Now the curious thing is that these two distinct worlds of interests, the secular and the eternal, were known by names derived from words which were once synonymous. This may help, to illustrate if not exactly to prove, one of the contentions in this book, namely that the dichotomy of the two worlds recognized by medieval Christendom and by much of traditional Christianity, has been in fact a false one, just as the traditional view of the dichotomy of man is invalid.

During the Middle Ages the two worlds of interests were theoretically in a happy state of complementary co-operation and mutual respect for each other's rightful authority. In practice, this was rather a state of truce, which from time to time broke down as either one or the other became dominant. But from the Renaissance onwards, the interests of the secular world have step by step been winning increasing emancipation from the interests of the eternal world, and at the same time secular pursuits have been growing in number and diversity. The reverse side of this picture is that the interests of the eternal world, in so far as they are identifiable with ecclesiastical practice and rule, have been steadily retreating. This process is secularization, i.e. the apparent victory of the secular world.

Let us take the example of education. In Europe it was the monasteries which kept alive what learning there was in the Dark Ages, and as the Middle Ages emerged, there grew out of these the first of the great European universities. They were founded for the study of theology, as the Divinity Hall still standing in Oxford so clearly illustrates to this day. Theology was seen, as the core of all sound learning. In the oldest universities the Faculty of theology still holds the place of honour. Wisdom began in the fear of the Lord, but reached out to all sound worthwhile human interests. The very idea of a university was that it should bring together all academic pursuits and give a man a completely balanced, an all-round, a universal education. Theology was the queen of the sciences, and these latter gradually began to emerge as individual disciplines.

From the Renaissance onwards, the young sciences struggled to get to their feet, and later, with the vigour of adolescents, they broke free from theological restraint and ecclesiastical control. Mother Church was overslow in recognizing the real worth of these rebellious young offspring which had come to birth in the very places of learning founded for the glory of God and the defence of the true faith. By the nineteenth century, universities were being founded which had no faculty of theology at all, and some had constitutions which declared that they were purely secular institutions in which no religious subjects could be pursued. The older universities began to abolish the required entrance examinations in Biblical knowledge and the necessity to give assent to Christian doctrines before matriculation was possible.

The same trend of secularization can be seen in general education. Literacy and education for all was largely pioneered by the church. From the Reformation onwards the availability of the Bible in the vernacular was in Protestant countries an added incentive to become literate. Even the Sunday School took its rise in a move to provide the elements of education for the working children of the poor on the only day they were free. Until this century primary education was mainly a matter of mastering the three R's, sometimes known as the four R's because religion figured pretty largely through the study of the Bible. Primary and secondary education then became increasingly secularized as they were taken over more and more by the state. Any religious or biblical teaching that is given at all is right out on the periphery. The great heritage of knowledge made available by the sciences and the modern 'knowledge explosion', determines the pattern and content of education today. The average adolescent of our day is being moulded by his education to take his place in secular society as a secular man.

What has been briefly described in the field of education can be paralleled in several other areas, all of which have been sometimes referred to as 'the lost provinces of religion'. The time was when the church was the only agent in society which concerned itself with the study of the nature of man and with the promotion of his spiritual health, but now there are other agents with similar concerns. Psychology—the study of the mind or human behaviour—is a secular science. Psychiatry—the art of healing the psyche or mind—is a secular pursuit. Social welfare, marriage counselling, various kinds of therapy designed to restore a person to the maximum mastery of his natural abilities, are often secular professions promoted by the state. The priest or pastor is sometimes confused today as to what constitutes his real role, for it seems so much more limited than it was in an earlier day when he was a 'father-in-god' to his flock in every possible way. This role seems so often today to be parcelled out to a number of specialists, usually working on a secular basis.

Let us now turn from the social changes which reflect secularization to the way in which it has changed what men think about the world and the life they live. We have already referred to the dualism of the two worlds in the medieval view. The supernatural world, though normally unseen, was believed to impinge upon the natural world at many points. An unusual or otherwise unexplainable event was readily interpreted as being caused by the unseen powers of the supernatural world. In popular thinking, evil spirits, ghosties, saints and guardian angels were conceived as carrying on an unseen war around one. Many processes which we now regard as quite natural and logical were mysteries to medieval man and consequently offered a ready seedbed for all kinds of explanations which depended upon intervention by some supernatural force.

But as the sciences began to develop, they gradually brought to light quite natural explanations for some aspects of observable phenomena which had previously been regarded as of supernatural origin. Unseen forces of a natural kind came to be recognized. To the ordinary man there is no obvious connection at all between the tides, the movement of the planets across the sky, and the falling of objects to the ground. It was a brilliant leap forward when Isaac Newton recognized that they can all be explained by the one force, which we now call gravity. He proceeded to enunciate in 1687 the inverse square of universal gravitation. This confirmed Kepler's three laws of planetary motion, which had so far been unexplained even though they correctly described how the planets moved. Knowledge of such laws as these made it much more difficult than before to contemplate the possibility even for God suddenly to cause a planet to behave in an irregular way, or to make stones fly up in the air instead of falling to the ground.

The areas of mystery, in some respects at least, seemed to be closing. There is a story told of how the famous astronomer Pierre Simon de Laplace was explaining to Napoleon his theory of the origin of the planets. When Napoleon asked him where in his theory he had left a place for God, he replied, "Sir, I have no need of that hypothesis." This is true of all the natural sciences. God is not a factor who has to be allowed for in their calculations. Now that kind of thinking about God which looks for evidence of His activity in phenomena which have no natural explanation is often referred to as a belief in the 'God of the gaps'. At the moment admittedly there are still many gaps in our knowledge, but the closing of so many gaps in everyday experience has meant that it needs no great stretch of the imagination to see that the gaps could readily close to the point where there is no room left for any faith in that kind of God.

The image of God as a supernatural being, who from time to time intervenes in the affairs of the natural world in clearly recognizable ways, and who can suspend or reverse the usual behaviour of natural phenomena, if He so wishes, in order to perform His will, is one which has become less and less tenable as the new world has emerged. As the sciences have moved from one apparent success to another, and paved the way for the rapid advance of technology, the ordinary man has felt more and more confident that he understands the natural forces and processes with some degree of certainty. And at the same time the sense of the supernatural which once weighed quite heavily with him has now receded, and plays a decreasing role in his thinking and experience.

Secularization is not simply something which divides men into two distinct classes—the secular and the religious. Practically all contemporary men show the marks of secularity in some form or another. The new secular man is in all of us to some degree. At the extremes only do we see two distinct classes. On the one hand there is the materialist who believes he has abandoned completely the religious heritage of the past, and on the other there is the conservative Christian believer, who believes he has resisted completely the inroads of secularization. (To the extent that he is still thinking within a framework of concepts which is far more medieval than contemporary, he is correct.) In between these two extremes there are many grades of secular man. The great mass of people of western culture still play at least lipservice to past religious traditions, but the proportion of their daily life that it directly influences grows increasingly less. Let us mention three examples.

In the first place man looks more and more for natural causes in the problems which beset him. If the potato crop fails, he does not regard it as an intervention by God to demonstrate His judgment—a judgment which must be accepted in humility and responded to with penitence and fasting. The natural causes are looked for, precautions are taken to prevent the calamity from spreading, and the most adequate remedies known are put into operation. Indeed in agriculture and in human and animal health, diseases are now forestalled wherever possible, by such methods as the application of trace elements to the soil, sterilization, a balanced diet and immunization.

This leads secondly to the fact that secular man neither expects nor believes in the miraculous intervention by God in the times of his desperate need. At this point the word 'miracle' needs to be more carefully analysed. The word originally meant a marvel, something which was so extraordinary as to attract attention, wonder and even awe. In this sense the word still has a valid meaning for us, since there are many things in our experience which make us marvel. The advent of television, penicillin, nuclear fission were all marvels. When modern surgery restores sight to a blind man, when a drunkard is reformed, when what appears to be certain catastrophe is averted, then the word 'miracle' arises naturally to our lips in order to describe them.

But if the word 'miracle' is used to describe a supernatural intervention by God, which is possible only through the temporary suspension of natural laws and forces, then we are talking about something else. It is this kind of definition which lies behind much popular talk of miracles. But it is a view of miracle which does not properly belong to the ancient world, where there was no clear understanding of permanent natural laws, and where they could distinguish only between the usual and the unusual. Certainly the Bible bears witness to the wonderful works of God, the signs and miracles of His grace, but it is anachronistic to read into these affirmations a much later understanding of miracle, one which belongs particularly to the medieval view of the interpenetration of the two worlds—the natural and supernatural. The receding of the sense of the supernatural world, characteristic of the secularizing progess, is bringing an end to that idea of miracle which implies a temporary suspension of natural law. We know that if the world is to avoid being thrown into the holocaust of a nuclear war, we must not look for a supernatural intervention in the form, say, of a regiment of angels. Men themselves must learn to handle their own passions. It is within the framework of natural forces that the miracles of God's grace will be recognized.

There have been periods when it has been popular to appeal to miracle as a means of proving the validity and truth of the Christian faith. Until only a hundred years ago the Gospel records of the 'miracles' of Jesus were regarded as one of the most telling ways of substantiating the divine powers of Jesus and hence the Christian claims about Him. But the historicity of the 'miracle' stories has now been severely undermined by modern Biblical study, which has shown that we have here no infallible historical records, but the testimony of Christian traditions which had been moulded by two or more generations of oral transmission. Even many of today's Christians, who in other respects may be regarded as being very liberal in their outlook, have been inclined to rest their faith on the historical reliability of the resurrection narratives, as pointing to at least one incontestable miracle of a supernatural character, and they have been alarmed when the 'Empty Tomb' stories came to be regarded as legendary. Even in the Easter affirmation of the Resurrection of Jesus, so important for Christianity, we can now point to no firm historical evidence to show that there occurred there a miracle which involved suspension or reversal of natural laws—in this case, the normal processes of decay into which the physical body enters after the point of death. The truth of the Resurrection of Jesus must be understood in terms other than these.

We shall take, as the third example of the influence of secularization, the practice and meaning of prayer. In a world where cause and effect have been shown to operate at so many more points than was earlier imagined, we are forced to ask to what extent prayers of petition and intercession which plead with God for the speedy fulfilment of certain clear objectives, really depend upon a belief in the 'God of the gaps'. To what extent can we believe any more that "The prayer of a righteous man has great power in its effects"? Secular man finds it hard to be convinced that there is a chain of cause and effect which follows a channel leading from the believer to God, and from God to the physical context to which the believer directed his prayer.

Some believers claim that their prayers have been marvellously answered. But there is never any way of showing that what they regarded as an answer would not have happened anyway. And when the particular answer the believer had in mind does not eventuate, then that which actually happened is interpreted by him as the answer God chose to give. This means that the believer knows from the outset that his prayer will be answered, and nothing that happens will convince him to the contrary. But at the same time it reduces 'answered prayer' to something like a meaningless statement.

Petition and answer should not, of course, be regarded as the sole content of Christian prayer, but in the popular mind this has often been the case, and it is just at this point that secularization has greatly undermined the practice of prayer, and has made the Christian much more cautious about the forms of his petitions and the areas in which they may be regarded as legitimate. One of the benefits of secularization in this field has been that it has shown up the fact that much that has passed for Christian prayer was in fact a form of magic, by which the Christian was attempting to operate supernatural forces to bring about his own ends, however laudable they might have been.

Finally it is to be noted that secularization is now spreading over the whole world. In the same way as it has undermined many aspects of the medieval form of Christianity, so it is affecting those civilizations which have grown up on the foundation of other religious faiths. The new secular man is being born in the Indian, the African and the Chinese as well as in the European. In Russia and China we find a particularly militant form of secularization which sees religious faith as an enemy to be fought and vanquished.

The world is today becoming in effect a smaller and more closely interdependent society. Communication, increased opportunities of travel, interchange of knowledge and forms of education all mean that, though the old cultural characteristics will linger on for a long time yet, there is already being sown the seed of a global culture. So far as we can see at the moment the chief characteristic of such a possible global culture will be its secularity. This is the one common element which is spreading everywhere.

From the time when the Pope divided the new geographical world between Spain and Portugal until the great missionary expansion of the nineteenth century, it was the firm belief of Christian Europe that the Christian religion of the European pattern must eventually encompass the earth. At the beginning of this century some Christians were hopefully raising the slogan "The evangelization of the world in our generation". But after some encouraging beginnings, particularly in Africa and in the Pacific, the great missionary expansion of the last two centuries has now ground down to a dead slow. The churches in Europe and in those countries where European culture was planted by early colonization, now find that they face a missionary situation at home. Within the last generation secularization has made greater inroads into the framework of Christian culture than in the previous three centuries, and it is still accelerating.

Out of the missionary movement there was born the Ecumenical Movement. This was slow at first, but since the Second World War, it has grown in strength, and has now taken root in the Roman Catholic Church—the largest and hitherto the most conservative church of the West. Many see in the Ecumenical movement the hope that the institutional Christianity of Europe will yet encircle the globe and provide the spiritual basis for the global culture. But has the Ecumenical Movement come one hundred years too late? For while ecumenical leaders strive to meet the challenge of the times by bringing together the living elements in their churches, they still find themselves weighed down as with chains by ecclesiastical machinery and dogmas of the past. By the time visible unity is restored to the church, the community of active committed Christians may have been reduced in size and influence to a quite insignificant island in a vast secular sea.

Secularization, as it is at present spreading and developing, is dividing the modern world into two. On the one hand there is an official and institutional form of Christianity seeking to be faithful to the beliefs and forms of Christendom's past glory, and on the other there is a secular, non-religious society which tends to assume that emancipation from all religious faith is part of the goal of complete secularization. This division, if allowed to continue, could prove more disastrous than the divisions to which the Reformation gave rise.

This division is a false one, first, because it fails to recognize that secularization originated in Christian Europe and not elsewhere. Admittedly not all the products of European culture have necessarily been of Christian origin, but before the church abandons secularization as if it were a foundling child, she must look more carefully to see if this is not Christianity's own offspring. For if it is (as later we shall try to show), then the church has the responsibility to guide the process of secularization forward and assist it to keep to its proper path, the very path whose beginning and direction are to be found in the Judeo-Christian heritage. The secularist who regards secularization as a matter of winning complete emancipation from the old heritage, is in fact turning secularism into an absolute, and without realizing it, he is in danger of becoming enslaved to a new form of idolatry. The present growing schism between the remnants of Christian orthodoxy and the secular world is a false one, which can lead both to ruin. This schism can be healed only if both are prepared to acknowledge the essential relationship between the Christian faith and secularization.

Then secondly, the church must realize that the influence of the Christian faith is not at all confined to the sphere of the organized church. It is often being said today that the church is back again in the first century situation. This is a dangerous half-truth. In the first century the church was a growing spreading minority in a completely non-Christian environment. Today the church is a diminishing minority in a cultural environment which has been largely shaped by its Christian past; and while orthodox Christianity is making only minor advances in Christian culture, the pattern of secularization to which it gave rise, is still spreading rapidly. It is rather paradoxical that while European political colonization is nowadays firmly rejected, the spread of European culture goes on apace in such forms as education, science and technology, democratic rule, and Western standards and ways of thought. Fewer and fewer people remain uninfluenced by the Christian faith, however slight it may appear on the surface, or however distorted the form of influence may be judged to be.

The old pattern of European Christendom with its complementary roles of state and church is fast disappearing. Secularization on a global scale is bringing in a new situation in which the Christian community and the secular society within which it lives, must both discover their proper mutual relationships. The Christian community in particular must be careful not to waste unnecessary energy fighting an enemy that her own misjudgment has largely created. Even the first disciples, St. Mark tells us, nearly fell into this error, and the Master said, "He that is not against us is for us."

CHAPTER 7

The New Theology

In what ways, if any, do the new views of the world and of man affect Christian theology? There are some who want to say that theology is little affected by these temporal matters, for it has to do with the timeless truths which have been revealed by God once and for all and which must therefore remain the same for ever. It is noticeable that such people are usually reluctant to admit that there *is* a new view of the Bible, a new view of the world or a new view of man. In other words they resolutely shut their eyes to the new world which is fast emerging around them.

On the other hand there are those who conclude, often reluctantly, that religion, theology and Christianity have come to the end of their course. Certainly, when we compare the story of the sciences with the story of theology over the last six hundred years, the latter looks rather like something from the *Looking-Glass* world of Alice. Six hundred years ago the sciences did not exist, two hundred years ago they were getting into their stride, today they seem to have the ball at their feet. But six hundred years ago theology seemed to have the ball at its feet, and felt that it knew a great deal about God, a hundred years ago it was ready to confess that there were *some* things about God it was not sure of, today theology wonders if it knows *anything* about God, and tomorrow, so some believe, theology will not even exist.

In between the two extremes there are those who want to be faithful to the heritage from the past, and at the same time take seriously the challenge of the new world. The attempt to reconcile these two did not start all at once, any more than the new world emerged all at once. The task has been accepted in academic theological circles for a long time, but only in the last few years has there been more popular and widespread interest in what is going on. Bishop John Robinson, as much as anyone, may be given the credit for breaking through the academic barrier and stimulating the so-called man in the street to take an interest in the contemporary theological task. The names of Rudolf Bultmann, Paul Tillich and Dietrich Bonhoeffer have now become quite widely known. It has led to the popular use of the term 'The New Theology'. This name (whether it is a good one or not is beside the point), raises a crucial question. If a theology relevant to the new world appears, and immediately is labelled 'new theology', how is one to judge whether it is the genuine successor to the more orthodox theology of the past? May it not be some sort of 'pretender', whose claim to be heir to the throne of the queen of the sciences is actually false?

Our first task is to discuss what theology is, and to distinguish it from several other things with which it is closely related, such as doctrine, Christian experience, and philosophy. The word 'theology' means the study or knowledge of God. But where does one start? If there were a body of fixed and permanent knowledge about God which He himself had already revealed, then theology would consist of the attempt to understand it and discuss it. Some people do think of theology in these terms. But we have seen that whatever Christians might have thought in the past, we can no longer say that we actually possess a body of knowledge which answers to this description, whether it be by revelation or by science. Not even the Bible can any longer be treated as if it were a quarry of timeless propositional truths to be mined like diamonds and then set in a gleaming diadem of Christian theology. Theology cannot therefore be defined as the study of the revealed knowledge of God, for there is none.

Neither is theology to be confused with philosophy. There have been times in the past when these two did seem very close. They are both intellectual disciplines dealing with the deepest questions of human existence, and when they were being pursued by men of Christian convictions, who were asking the same kind of questions, they were not easy to separate. But many of the questions about which men used to philosophize have now become disciplines of study in their own right. One of the earlier names for the sciences was simply 'natural philosophy'. Nowadays philosophy mainly sees its task as one of assisting other disciplines to think clearly and meaningfully about their particular areas of study. Philosophy has aided theology a good deal within this century in helping it to examine its own language critically, and there is still an important place for philosophizing about the nature of religious experience, and the reality of religious truth. But theology is not the same as philosophy, for theology has its own distinct area of study and that is the Christian faith itself.

Now whereas any honest clear thinker can be a philosopher of some kind, no one can be a theologian (we are here confining ourselves to the Christian religion) who has not already embraced the Christian faith himself. In doing this he has professed the Christian faith as a reality in his own life and he has committed himself to some form of Christian obedience. It is at this point that we see the clear relationship between theology and Christian experience. But whereas all theologians must be Christian by profession of faith, not all professing Christians are theologians. It could be said of course that whenever a Christian is making an honest attempt to think out some problem connected with his Christian faith, then he is taking the first steps in theology. The only difference between him and the professional theologian is that the latter is pursuing the problem at that greater depth which the tools of an academic discipline make possible.

But how does the Christian go about thinking his way through his theological problem? Well, first of all he turns to the source of his faith. He became a Christian (or, alternatively, chose to be confirmed in that in which he had been nurtured from infancy) because of the influence of the Christian heritage, guarded and proclaimed by the Christian church. He is bound to study that heritage for himself. It takes him first and foremost to the Bible, which is the definitive witness to the period of origins. Then he turns to the long story of the church and the history of Christian thought. The latter has become crystallized in creeds and confessions, and in the most widely accepted writings of the theologians of the past. All this is sometimes referred to as Christian doctrine. But just as the Bible must be understood within its own historical context, as we have already seen, so all Christian creeds and writings of the past must be related to their own time. They reflect the period in which they were written, not only in the common presuppositions of men of that time, but in the kind of questions then being asked.

But we live in our own historical context, and we are concerned with our own questions and with those of our fellow-men. These are not necessarily the same as those of past ages, for history is always bringing change. While the theologian is bound to take seriously the heritage of the Christian witness and thought of the past, that is only half of his task. In the light of this heritage he must think through the meaning of Christian faith and obedience afresh from the standpoint of the contemporary context in which he finds himself. If theology merely consisted of summarizing the affirmations and thoughts of the Christians of past ages, an electronic computer could be designed to do it better. Theology must always be a fresh living expression coming from the lips of Christian believers who are keenly aware of the problems and questions of their own time.

It is thus possible to define theology quite simply as the attempt of the Christian to think about his faith and experience, to test it in the light of the past heritage, and to relate it to all the knowledge and experience of his own time. The theologian then finds himself at a point of tension, where he is trying to reconcile the 'old' and the 'new', i.e. the old heritage and the new questions and knowledge. If theology is genuine and alive, it is always new, for in each new generation it is taking as its starting point a new historical context. The more the historical context changes, the harder and more demanding becomes the theological task, and the more likely it is that the living theology that comes out of that period will be labelled the 'New Theology'.

The theologian must try to steer his ship between the dangers of Scylla and Charybdis. If he answers the contemporary questions in a way which does not do justice to the heritage of the past, his 'new' theology may no longer qualify as *Christian* theology. If he faithfully affirms the answers given by the theologians of the past, but does not come to grips with contemporary questions, he is not expressing a Christian *theology*, and his words will be increasingly passed by as irrelevant. There is no theological radar or automatic pilot to which he can turn over the responsibility for steering the straight path. Whether by nature he leans to the conservative right or the liberal left, he must steer his craft by faith alone.

Let us briefly look at some of the periods of the past where this tension caused by concern for both the old and new has been most acute. First of all it is reflected in the Bible itself. The opening two chapters give us two different expressions of the beginning of things. The older one is now in chapter two and reflects the comparatively simple world view of the semi-nomad of the early second millennium B.C. The later account, now in the first chapter, reflects the more sophisticated world view of the time of the Assyrian and Babylonian Empires. The Jewish scholars who put the first five books together during the fifth century B.C. preserved for us both the old story and the new story and placed them side by side. This blending of the old version and the new version is to be found in many places in the Old Testament.

The problem of the old and the new came critically to the fore in the advent of Jesus of Nazareth. The Jewish community to which he belonged was by now so wedded to the written form of the old heritage, that it could not tolerate the thought of a new prophet, proclaiming something new. Jesus is reported to have countered the charge that he was abandoning the ancestral Jewish heritage by saying, "Do not suppose that I have come to abolish the Law and the prophets; I did not come to abolish, but to complete. I tell you this; so long as heaven and earth endure, not a letter, not a stroke, will disappear from the Law until all that must happen has happened." On the other hand the Gospel of Matthew in the very same chapter portrays Jesus as one who clearly recognized that there was something new in what he said, for we have the repeated words from his mouth, "You have learned that they were told . . . But what I tell you is this . . ."

The tension between the old and the new continued to mark the life of the church in her first two centuries. It was no easy task to reconcile the old with the new. It is all too easy to assume that Jesus in his teaching entrusted the content of Christian theology to his disciples, and that the task of theology thereafter was simply to 'contend for the faith which was once for all delivered to the saints'. This is far from the truth. It was not the teaching of Jesus which became the focal point of the Christian faith, but the person and activity of Jesus himself. The first one to hammer out anything like a theology of the Christian faith was Paul, and curiously enough he appears never to have met the flesh and blood Jesus of Nazareth, let alone to have heard his teaching on the 'Kingdom of God' direct from his lips.

Not all Christians of the mid-first century agreed with the way in which Paul saw the 'old' consummated in the 'new', as his letters to the Galatians and the Romans make clear. Although Paul's theology was destined to be the dominant model for all later Christian thinking, it is fortunate that the New Testament preserves for us some other embryonic theological patterns, notably the Johannine writings which go so far as to express this theology in the form of speeches attributed to Jesus. There were other interpretations of the person of Jesus which were never caught up in the main stream of Christian development, and later died out, but the fact that this amount of diversity of thought was eventually included in the New Testament shows the willingness of the church to hold in suspension varying and sometimes conflicting viewpoints.

Even in the second century when the rift between Christianity and Judaism had become wide and permanent, the church was still wrestling with the problem of how to reconcile the new Gospel centred on Jesus Christ with the old heritage inherited from Israel. When there was a spirited move on the part of some to cut Christianity off from its Israelite origins completely, and abandon the Old Testament as Jewish scriptures, the church resolutely rejected it. On the contrary the church moved to the point where it accepted as its Bible both the *Old* Testament and the *New* Testament. Nothing could demonstrate more clearly than this, the determination of the Christian community to hold together in tension both the old and the new.

And there *is* a tension in the Bible. The church has never been quite sure what to make of the Old Testament. On the one hand there have been various ingenious attempts made during the centuries to resolve the tension in the Bible by trying to make it say the same thing in all its parts. On the other hand voices have been raised, as again in this century, which say that the tension should be eased by jettisoning the Old Testament.

After the first five centuries had witnessed a succession of theological controversies, the point was reached where a pattern of Christian thought was formulated which was destined to serve the church well for many centuries. But time does not stand still, and, with its passing, new experiences and new questions press themselves upon the life of the church. Such a time was the thirteenth century when there arrived at the newly emerging universities of Europe some of the teaching of the ancient Greek thinkers, Aristotle in particular. This stimulated considerable interest in academic circles and also a little alarm. It became a question whether Christian thought could assimilate the new learning. Full credit must be given to St. Thomas Aquinas (*c.* 1225–74), who, building upon the work of his teacher Albertus, constructed such a magnificent synthesis of traditional Christian doctrine and of the new knowledge that it became the standard expression of Christian doctrine for the Roman Catholic Church up until the present day.

The only other period of theological ferment which we need refer to here is that of the sixteenth century Reformation. It is rather paradoxical that those who are most inclined to idolize the Reformation period seem to be among the very ones who are most suspicious of the winds of theological change which are blowing in our own day. It is true that the Reformation was chiefly concerned with a few very relevant though central issues, and that many affirmations and presuppositions of Christian orthodoxy remained undisturbed. At the same time in the eyes of the Catholic theologians of that time, reformed theology appeared to be a 'new theology', which deserved to be rejected just on those grounds. But there was one important principle that emerged that is particularly relevant to our discussion: that the readiness to recognize that no reformation of Christian doctrine can ever be final. The *ecclesia* which is genuinely *reformata* is *semper reformanda*. Reformation is a continuing process, and this applies as much to Christian thought as to Christian practice and ecclesiastical structure.

In the light of these glimpses into the fluid state of Christian theology in times past, and the tension the theologian has felt between the demands of present experience and faithfulness to the past heritage, we now turn to try and appreciate the task of theology in our own day. When one considers the magnitude and radical nature of the questions posed for the theologian by the new world, it is not surprising to find that theologians are beginning to speak about a new reformation more radical than that of the sixteenth century.

For if the theological task can be defined in terms of facing the tension between the old and the new, then it is only to be expected that both the speed and the extent of the change, in which we are at present all caught up, will inevitably bring changes in theological expression greater than at any earlier period in Christian history. It is fair to say that the world has changed more in the last hundred years than in the previous eighteen hundred. Until a little over a hundred years ago men were using the same means of travel as had been used for several millennia—the horse by land and the sail-boat by water. Education was still the privilege of the few. Today travel and communication have reached speeds and diverse forms which were unthinkable a century ago. Universal education is rapidly spreading and reaching ever higher standards. Medical practice has changed completely. It is said that something like ninety-five per cent of all scientists who have ever lived, are still alive. This is the kind of world that the theologian lives in and to which he must relate the faith by which he lives and the Christian heritage which has been entrusted to him. Is it any wonder that theology is today in a more fluid state than at any time since the period of Christian origins?

In the previous chapters we have already noted some of the specific questions which the new world is forcing us to ask with a new sense of urgency. Let us turn to what could be regarded as the most fundamental question of all theology. What reality lies behind the word 'God'?

We start with a sketch of the mental image conveyed by the word 'God' in the world view which obtained in Christendom before the new world began to emerge. This can not be fully appreciated without remembering the complete supernatural world which was thought to lie beyond this visible world, and which had such an overpowering reality for the medieval mind. Heaven and hell, along with those who dwelt in them, were conceived in spatial terms. Although they were beyond the stars, or under the earth, they were thought to be places just as real, and certainly more lasting, than the earth on which men live. Besides the souls of the departed who were thought to reside in one or other of these two places, there were varieties of angels and immortal beings which were thought to have peopled heaven since the time of creation.

It was from within this spatial heaven, far above and yet real, not of the temporal quality of earth and yet within space, that God ruled both heaven and earth from a golden throne. There is little doubt that in the human imagination he was pictured in the form of a man, and thus the painters often portrayed him. While some may have wondered what was the most adequate way of attempting to portray the Holy Trinity, the risen Lord Jesus is described by the two most ancient creeds as sitting on the right hand of God the Father, and so it naturally led to a mental picture in which the three 'persons' of the Trinity were pictured as individual forms though acting in unison. This whole picture of the Lord God in His heaven all hangs together very well, and readily wins a response from the mind of the believing Christian.

But what happens when this heavenly world is caused bit by bit to disintegrate and lose its reality? For that is exactly what has happened over the last four hundred years, as all the aspects of the new world have been slowly impressing themselves upon man. The new world view of space made it steadily clearer that this supernatural world could not be located any more in some distant space area of the universe. By last century men were preparing to eliminate a personal devil, and were inclining to the view that a hell of eternal punishment was hardly consistent with the goodness of God. Then the ministering spirits and angels began to recede into the background and lose their former reality. This left a very indistinct picture of the disembodied souls of the departed, conceived as being in the presence of God, in some rather vague existence still called heaven.

But since the new view of man has virtually deprived the concept of a disembodied soul of any meaningful reality, it means that the medieval picture becomes further simplified to the plain affirmation that God is in His heaven. (This, incidentally, is much closer than the medieval picture to the Biblical understanding of heaven.) But now we must ask to what extent the common conception of God itself derives from the same kind of projection of the human consciousness out into the unknown, as that which initiated animism, Platonism and the doctrine of immortality. Plato did in fact speak of God as the great soul. But if we can no longer accept the reality of a disembodied human soul, then what does it mean to attribute consciousness, thinking powers, will and emotions to a non-physical bodiless being, however greatly exalted? When Bishop Robinson startled the world in 1963 with the headlines of an article "Our image of God must go!" he was simply putting into plain words something that theologians had been recognizing for some time.

The fact is that while the medieval picture is still held with conviction by some, for many others the image of God as a supernatural being has already gone. On the assumption that God must be defined as 'a supernatural being', it has led some to atheism as the only alternative. Increasing numbers have become agnostic, in that they do not profess to know what the basic realities of man's world are, and are unprepared either to affirm or to deny that one called God is a reality.

Here we must hasten to point out that among Christian thinkers over the centuries the conception of God has varied considerably more in expression than is often popularly supposed, and theologians have always wanted to guard themselves against the implications of such crude and concrete images of God as may have been prevalent in the popular imagination. Here for example is how John Scotus Erigena (*c.* 810–877), a deeply original thinker and a great scholar, long before our time expressed his concept of God in the words of a prayer:

> O thou who art the everlasting Essence of things beyond space and time and yet within them; O thou who dost transcend and yet pervade all things, manifest thyself to us as we feel after thee, seeking thee in the dark places of our ignorance.

Theologians have always recognized, to some degree, that one can never talk about God with the preciseness that is possible with tangible objects. For this reason it has been acknowledged that human language, evolved for communication in and about the finite world, will always be inadequate for discussion of the infinite God. In particular it has been realized that when terms drawn from human experience and personality are applied to God, they must inevitably be metaphorical and symbolic in character.

But while this has always been so, it is fair to say that today theologians are more aware than ever before of the tentative and symbolic nature of all talk about God. In the new view of the Bible we see one of the main reasons for this. Now that the Bible must be regarded as the witness of ancient men to what *they believed* God was saying and doing in their own day, and not the verbatim revelation spoken by God Himself, then even the biblical language is relative to its age and cannot be appealed to as if it were God's very own words about Himself. Nor is it sufficient just to say that religious language is symbolic. How is one to show that there *is* some unseen and intangible reality to which the God-talk refers by means of symbols?

In the past there has been no real need to show that God-talk is meaningful, for belief in some kind of supernatural reality was then a common premise that could be taken for granted. This is no longer the case. T. S. Eliot has put it clearly:

> But it seems that something has happened that has never happened before;
> though we know not just when, or why, or how, or where.
> Men have left GOD not for other gods, they say, but for no god;
> and this has never happened before.

It is important to appreciate this new situation. It is not just a question of an isolated rebellious individual proclaiming defiantly, "There is no God". In earlier days he could be written off as a fool. But today, for reasons discussed in earlier chapters, it is simply a widespread cultural phenomenon that for increasing numbers the God-talk and religious language in which the church proclaims her message possesses little or no reality. It is ceasing to be part of the common language and cultural presuppositions. Before the emergence of the new world the church proclaimed her message in what was already a religious context, no matter where she turned. The advent of secularization has meant that the traditional religious language of the church has now become a specialist language which to many in the secular world is not meaningful, and indeed even non-sense.

What is the church to do in this new cultural situation? By and large the church has been reluctant to venture far away from its traditional language because of the conviction that certain fundamental terms and concepts are indispensable to the Christian faith, and if the world does not want to try to understand them, then it is so much the worse for the world. It wants to affirm that God has revealed Himself in such and such terms in the Bible and in the life of the church, and men have the choice of responding to or rejecting the Gospel in this form, for there is no other. Karl Barth (1886–) is the most outstanding contemporary exponent of this 'revelational' theology. For him the revelation of God as attested by Scripture stands over against contemporary human culture, whether religious or secular, with the divine Word of promise and judgment.

There are other Christian thinkers who believe that the new cultural situation must be taken a lot more seriously. Paul Tillich (1886–1965), for example, has tried to break out of the traditional language and discuss God and the Christian faith in terms that are still common to all men whether secular or religious. He has interpreted the meaning of the word 'God' in terms of man's ultimate concern. "This does not mean that first there is a being called God and then the demand that man should be ultimately concerned about him. It means that whatever concerns a man ultimately becomes god for him, and, conversely that a man can be concerned ultimately only about that which is god for him."

A few have startled the Christian world by going even further. They believe we are in the process of entering a post-theistic age, in which the word 'God' by reason of all its past associations is becoming increasingly irrelevant and there is no possibility of, nor even any point in attempting to salvage it. In this present decade they have been called the "Death of God" theologians. Some of them speak of the death of God as if it were an event that has taken place in our time; others simply avoid the word 'God'. Paul van Buren, in his book *The Secular Meaning of the Gospel* has given us an interpretation of the Christian faith which does not depend upon the use of the word 'God' at all.

Naturally many Christians regard this extreme form of the contemporization of the Christian faith as such a radical departure from Christian orthodoxy as to be something quite different, and perhaps they are right. But on the other hand, if the church insists on speaking to the secular world in its own traditional 'religious' language, it is possible that the Christian faith will be written off as irrelevant to the new world, and will fade away as a cultural force. Such are the issues of theology today.

So far we have been concerned to try to state and appreciate the nature and the gravity of the questions which the new world poses for the Christian faith. We have as yet made no attempt to meet these challenges. To this task we shall presently turn. But at this point there is one final thing to be said. Whether we are Christians, agnostics or atheists, we are all involved in the present cultural crisis. For two reasons at least, the present ferment in Christian thought is, at the same time, of widespread significance for the total human situation.

Firstly, it is true that the new world has challenged at many points the validity of the traditional Christian answers to such basic questions as: What is man? Where did he come from? What is he here for? Where is he going? But no scientist, philosopher, or secular prophet has supplied alternative answers. Here and there the quest of man for the ultimate answers has given rise to a certain resurgence of religion, both Christian and non-Christian, both orthodox, and more often, unorthodox. In some areas the communist ideology has, temporarily at least, given men something to live for. But secular man for the most part is left with his questions unanswered, sometimes still hopeful, as with the humanist, sometimes despairing as in some forms of art. Sometimes he does not know what is causing his unease, and sometimes he is aware of the God-shaped vacuum in his life.

Secondly, it must be acknowledged that it was out of Christendom that the new world emerged. To understand the new world we must go back to the seeds and roots from which it sprang. Perhaps we shall find that just as the continued vitality and fruitfulness of the tree depends on the nourishment it receives from its roots, so the new world depends more than is realized on the nourishment it receives from its cultural roots. If the new world turns its back on the past heritage it may find itself to be like an uprooted tree, which will wither and die, and cultural thorns and thistles will spring up where once it proudly stood. And over the withering tree will be heard those puzzling words:

> For to him who has will more be given, and he will have abundance; but from him who has not, even what he has will be taken away.

PART II

The Biblical Origins of the New World

CHAPTER 8

The Mythological World of Ancient Man

To understand and meet the challenge of the new world we must turn back to examine the roots of the Christian heritage. This leads us to the Bible, the definitive witness to the faith of our fathers during its long formative period. But the Bible we have seen, must be studied against the background of its own original context in the ancient world. Until this century little was known of the ancient world before 500 B.C. except that which is contained in the Bible. We must now take time to sketch the outlines of the world of man in the ancient Middle East since this formed the immediate background for the people of Israel who gave us the Old Testament.

As ancient man surveyed his world, he found himself surrounded on all sides with movement and change, not only in fellow-humans, animals and birds, but in running water, scudding clouds, heavenly bodies travelling across the sky, rising dust-storms, the occasionally quaking earth and the vegetation which sprang up, flowered, fruited and died. Wherever there was movement there was life. Wherever there was life, there was evidently something corresponding to what he knew in himself, such as his own consciousness, his will and his emotions. He saw personality or personal life everywhere. The world to him was not an 'It', but a vast, powerful and complicated 'Thou'.

This means that when he tried to understand what he saw, and give some kind of explanation for the life and movement he witnessed, it did not occur to him to look for an abstract principle or a natural law. He was not interested in asking *how* a thing happened. That did not even appear to him to be a problem. He saw with his own eyes *how* a thing happened. What he wanted to know was *who* was behind the action. Everything that happened was thought to be willed by someone or other, and because this was the cause of the action, he would have thought it foolish and naïve to look for a simple explanation which would hold good on all such occasions. The person who had caused the action might well will one thing at one time and something different the next, just as he himself could vary his action to suit his mood.

But who were the persons whose actions he believed he was witnessing? Here, of course, no one ancient individual ever had to start off from scratch and puzzle it out for himself. Once human language had developed, ancient man was always the recipient of the heritage of oral tradition. He received this from his fathers and passed it on to his children with perhaps only very little change. But there was always room for a little change and that is how the heritage of ancient ideas of the world was gradually built up.

The oral tradition he received (and this all helped to make him the civilized man he was becoming) had already created names for the large number and varied kinds of personal forces who made his world such a live place. The names varied from one culture to another, as did also the kind of person or being that they represented. Fundamentally they were all 'spirits'. In most languages the word 'spirit' was derived from, or was still identical with the word for 'wind' or 'breath'. Since the wind can be seen by what it does and yet remains unseen, and since continued breathing is the best way of testing between the living person and the dead body, these words were the obvious ones for ancient man to use to describe the unseen personal forces at work.

But there are many diverse movements and forms of life in the world, and this naturally became reflected in the types of beings man came to recognize. There were major ones whom he called gods and goddesses, some with quite wide dominion, and others with clearly defined roles. There were also local spirits, good and bad, some of them puckish but harmless, some to be feared, some to be welcomed for their kindly aid.

Ancient man thus recognized himself to be in a very complex world, only one portion of which was visible to the naked eye. There was a whole intercourse of personal dealings going on in the world around him, just as real, even though unseen, as what was going on in the neighbouring village of the next valley hidden for the moment by the intervening hills. These personal spiritual forces placed man at a disadvantage just because they were unseen. Ancient man was at their mercy, and it was in his own interests to win and retain their favour. He inherited from the past the knowledge of the best methods of achieving this end. Any new methods he picked up in the course of his own experience were stumbled upon by accident, rather than discovered by venturesome experiment, for it did not pay to wander far from the known way.

In his encounter with this complex world, ancient man attributed equal reality to all his experiences. For him there was no absolute distinction to be made between dreams, hallucinations, and the impressions he received during the hours of wakefulness. The voices he heard and the people he saw were all equally real whether they were in dreams or daily life. In *his* dreams no doubt, as in ours, the strangest things happened, but then the whole world was to him a mysterious place where wonders abounded, and where nothing was impossible.

Now we must take his understanding of the spirits of the unseen world a stage further. They formed a whole community on their own, and this divine society he pictured in his imagination after the pattern of his own human society. Some of the social affairs of this spiritual society impinged upon his own visible part of the world, and some of them went on wholly in the unseen. Since these spiritual powers were personal, with wills and passions like our own, they loved, quarrelled, fought and entered into intrigue. All these doings he expressed in the form of stories which today we call myths. ('Myth' was simply the Greek word for any story told by word of mouth.)

What we nowadays know about dreams and the subconscious can help us understand in part how these myths came to be created. We know that dreams result from the various emotional conflicts which arise in us as a result of our daily experiences. Although in sleep we have temporarily lost consciousness, our mind goes on wrestling with these conflicts at lower or subconscious levels of mental activity. These lower levels do not deal with abstract concepts as readily as does the more highly developed stream of consciousness, and so the various factors of the conflict are translated into more objective symbols. The dream may take the form of a drama where people known to the dreamer play the parts of the ideas and concepts included in the particular conflict.

Perhaps in this process we have some hint as to the way in which the mind of ancient man, less adept in handling abstract concepts, was led to express the conflicts he felt among the unseen forces about him in the form of stories of the gods and spirits. In many ways these stories were a projection of the conflicts aroused in his own mind by his confrontation with the world he experienced. It is unlikely that any of the stories in the form in which they have come down to us were created by one man. Instead, they were a gradual development as an original theme was filled out and extended by successive generations. The comparative study of the myths of the ancient Middle East shows that the myths were in a continuous process of development and adaptation.

It is important to realize that, unlike our situation today, the mind of ancient man enjoyed almost unlimited freedom in developing the story. He lived in a world in which almost anything seemed possible. Once again we have a parallel in our dream experiences, where the subconscious mental processes are freed from the monitoring influence of an informed sophisticated consciousness, ever ready to bring a halt to any idea too outlandish by saying, "Don't be ridiculous. That's impossible." But when we wake we may recall the most outlandish dreams we have had. So it was with ancient man. In his case there was no body of accepted knowledge of the seen world to confine and actually hamper the processes of his imagination by impressing upon him what was really possible. Many of the ancient myths, like our dreams, are marked by the complexity of the plot and sub-plots, the lack of consistency in the characters and their actions, and the introduction, without warning, of further players in the cosmic drama.

In such an intellectual climate as that, some of the mythical interpretations of observable phenomena given by ancient man would have seemed to him much more obvious and common sense than our modern explanations, should it ever have been possible to present the latter to him for the purpose of choosing between them. For example, he experienced the same physical sense impressions as we do when witnessing the breaking of a drought by means of a violent storm. But our meteorological explanation in terms of barometric pressure, temperature and wind movements would have struck him as too abstract and remote to explain anything. Was it not clear that the hot wind that had been scorching the crops was the hot breath of the angry Heavenly Bull, which had now met its match with the arrival of the gigantic bird whose immense widespread wings were already darkening the sky and blotting out the light of the sun?

The process of myth-making has been called "the intellectual adventure of ancient man". But it was not simply an intellectual exercise, far less a form of entertainment, for ancient man knew himself to be involved in the processes of life and divine encounter which he saw all around him. Most of the myths which have come down to us in written form were not just stories or explanations of phenomena. They were part of a cultic activity and were associated with ritualistic acts, religious ceremonials, sacred dancing, and drama. It was in these media that ancient man played his part in the world scene, and responded in that way which he believed to be most appropriate to the occasion, and which would further promote his welfare.

Let us take, for example, his response to the changing seasons. He could not help but notice that the spring brought new life both in the fields and among the flocks. The cereals and fruit-trees quickly grew until they flowered and reached maturity in grain and fruit. But then the signs of life began to depart, and, as autumn fell, it was just as if the whole world was coming to a standstill in the state of death. How could he be sure that the annual cycle would start up all over again? There had been handed down to him a pattern of ritual which was believed to ensure that it would. In any case he knew that some seasons were better than others, and it was clear to him that this meant that at some times the gods were more pleased with his response than at others. So to ensure the return of the spring and to promote a successful and plentiful season he sought to win the favour of the gods concerned, by playing his traditional part in the cultic ritual.

This varied from one ancient culture to another but was performed in the late autumn, the winter solstice, or the early spring. In the Babylonian New Year Festival their creation myth was recited and partly acted out. This was a long involved story of how Marduk was elected King of the gods in order to attack and defeat Tiamat the goddess of the watery deep, who was spreading chaos by spawning all sorts of evil creatures. After the victory Marduk brought order out of chaos, cut the dead body of Tiamat in two to make heaven and earth, and so created a fit place for the gods to dwell in. The creation myth was deemed appropriate at the New Year because it was thought that before the return of spring life was possible, the basic creative act had to be performed afresh.

A common theme of the myths of the ancient cultures was the death and resurrection of the god of fertility. In Babylonia it was Tammuz, in Syria Adonis, in Egypt Osiris, in Canaan Baal, in Greece Persephone, whose death was marked by the falling leaves of autumn, whose imprisonment in the underworld of death explained the winter, and whose release by the gods of the underworld for one reason or another made possible the spring revival.

Now that we have briefly sketched the role of myth and ritual in the ancient world we can see why it is convenient to use the label 'mythological' to describe the world of ancient man. It is used in this book to refer generally to ancient man's distinctive way of looking at and responding to his world. For this reason it is important to see that we shall be using the word 'myth' in a somewhat different sense. They are related in that the mythological world view of ancient man was expressed in the form of stories or myths, but it shall be argued later that there is something more permanently valid in 'myth' than in what has been here called the 'mythological'.

The reason for this is that there is a strong link between myth and poetry in that they both derive from the fertility of the human imagination as man makes his response to his environment at the deepest level. But whereas ancient man drew no clear dividing line between objective knowledge and the insights to be expressed in poetry, this is something we are forced to do. In the new world the mythological world view of ancient man is obsolete, but poetry is not obsolete. While it is true that myth is no longer appropriate for the objective understanding of natural phenomena, it may still have a valid role to play for the expression of man's sense of mystery and wonder in the world in which he finds himself. In both myth and poetry there is a freer and more fruitful use of words and concepts than prose, logic, or scientific description would allow.

We shall now summarize the chief characteristics of the mythological world of ancient man. Firstly, the whole cosmos was subject to a cyclic rhythm, The natural alternation of day and night, the waxing and waning of the moon, the yearly round of the seasons, the succession of one generation by the next, all led ancient man to a cyclic view of time. In cycles of different length he saw himself returning to an earlier point. This meant there could be no such thing as permanent progress and development; there could be only successive periods of growth and decay. The gods and men were all involved in this cyclic rhythm. We are used to the cyclic rhythm in the daily, monthly and annual routine, but we have become so conditioned to the sense of history in terms of a continuous line in which the past recedes ever further away, that we find it difficult to appreciate the time-world of ancient man.

Secondly, the mythological world was inevitably polytheistic. It was the meeting place and often the battle ground of a whole host of divine forces. Sometimes one major god might be thought of as having won the ascendancy, and then he became a king of the gods, but often there was no clear unity or system. The unseen world of the divine mirrored in many ways the human world, and the gods displayed all the same emotions and craftiness. It may be said that man was in effect working out the problems and conflicts he saw in his visible environment by projecting them into the divine figures which symbolized them.

Thirdly, the mythological world was divided into two parts, the unseen world of the gods, often associated with the sky above, and the visible tangible world to which men were confined. The gods could move freely about both parts and frequently did. They could break into men's affairs when they wished, and they could keep to themselves when they desired privacy from the inquisitive eye of man. The gods were thought for the most part to be very jealous of the advantages which their divine immortality gave them over the limitations of mortal man. It was natural that men should look up with envy to the unseen world of the gods, and the search for a method to become like the gods and to win immortality became a common theme in the myths which expressed their longings. Ancient man thus showed a strong tendency to develop an other-worldly look, and to depreciate the importance and significance of the tangible world in which he lived.

Fourthly, the unseen spiritual world around him so dominated the life of ancient man that the cultic practices of sacrifice and ritual, by which he sought to win the favour of the gods, were of paramount importance. Religion and religious practices embraced everything, whether it was family affairs, agriculture, politics or war. Religious practices showed a strong tendency to become stereotyped and unchangeable, and this had the effect of imprisoning man in an intricate network or pattern of behaviour, inherited from the past, from which he could not escape. That which originated in an attempt to win for him such elements of freedom as divine favour could bestow, ended by becoming a taskmaster.

Such was the way in which ancient man saw his world. The Bible presents the story of Israel from the lips of her own thinkers, prophets and witnesses, and shows how she believed herself to be called out from this ancient world to pioneer a new and distinctive way for the whole human race. In the succeeding chapters we shall examine the distinctive marks of the Judeo-Christian heritage, as they come to light when the Bible is studied against the background of the mythological world of ancient man. And we shall try to show that much that has come to a flowering in the new world has its roots in that rich heritage.

CHAPTER 9

The Concern with History and the End of Mythology

When we turn from the mythological world of ancient man to the Old Testament we find ourselves in a different world. It is a great pity that the casual Bible reader almost inevitably reads the Old Testament against the background of a sophisticated modern world, for then the first things to strike him are characteristics which are strange to him just because they reflect the ancient period. What he ought to find striking are some things which he usually never notices to be there, for the simple reason that they have become part and parcel of the modern world, and he does not realize, as he ought, that he has in fact inherited them from ancient Israel.

The mythological world of ancient man forms the real background for the appreciation of the Old Testament, and the first thing which strikes one is that the Old Testament contains so much writing of history. This historical concern in the Christian Bible still makes it unique among the holy books of the world. In the Holy Scriptures of Zoroastrianism, Hinduism, Buddhism or Islam, one finds no real interest in history at all, but in both the Old Testament and the New Testament the thread of history provides the framework and focal points.

Today we take a sense of history for granted. We know that the past has gone for ever and that the present moment can never be recaptured. We know that history brings change. All our thinking and our human endeavours, whether individual or collective, religious or secular, are pursued within a context of history, in which we are ever moving away from an original beginning, and nearer to some future goal.

But in the mythological world ancient man had not developed a sense of history. He saw himself as a creature of nature, and almost the plaything of the gods who controlled nature. The world moved in cycles of various frequencies, returning to the points it had passed before. So man's true welfare was chiefly to be attained by reconciling his life to the cycles of nature, such as day and night, summer and winter, death and rebirth. The really significant things were all executed by the unseen forces. The actions of men were of no great moment and indeed had little meaning.

How did the sense of history begin? It is generally agreed that it is of comparatively recent origin, and the beginnings of the writing of history are commonly traced back to the Greek historians Herodotus (*c.* 484–24 B.C.) and Thucydides (*c.* 460–400 B.C.). Herodotus is often called the 'Father of History' because he wrote a history of the Persian invasion of Greece after travelling extensively through the Middle East.

But Israel's concern with history takes us back at least five centuries earlier. Paul Schubert, in a symposium devoted to the *The Idea of History in the Ancient Near East* writes: "When it comes to the idea of history, it must be said that Israel, through its sacred scripture . . . has proved to be the strongest and most influential single force observable by the historian in shaping the idea of history throughout two millennia of Western history." The Cambridge historian, H. Butterfield, has said of the Old Testament "Altogether we have here the greatest and most deliberate attempts ever made to wrestle with destiny and interpret history and discover meaning in the human drama; above all to grapple with the moral difficulties that history presents to the religious mind."

We can hardly expect the Old Testament to tell us explicitly how Israel came to have a sense of history, for she was not given to think in abstract terms and did not have a language suited for it. Indeed Israel had no word even for 'history', the nearest Hebrew expression meaning simply 'the things of the days'. It is only by indirect means that we can learn how it all began. In the early stages, it was not at all easy to distinguish clearly the sense of history from the mythological context out of which it was emerging. Indeed, there was a strong tussle between the historical and the mythological concerns and this has continued in some degree down to the present day.

In the Old Testament there are two main complexes of historical material. The first is the Pentateuch, which sets out to sketch the history of the world from the day of creation to the point where Israel was about to enter the promised land. We now know that we cannot treat this material as if it had been written under the conditions that a modern historian would impose, namely, access to reliable contemporary records. But the remarkable thing is that these books betray a marked sense of history. They are expressed in terms of linear history and not in nature cycles. It was a pioneering feat of simply outstanding quality, testimony for which is seen in the fact that it served as the basic text-book of early human history for more than two and a half thousand years.

Modern scholarship has analysed the Pentateuch into at least four different strata, which were once independent, but which were at later stages blended together to form the present unity. The earliest of these may have come from about the time of Solomon. The unknown writer responsible for it (often referred to as the Yahwist) appears to have sifted through the myths, legends and stories that had been transmitted orally by his forefathers, and to have moulded them into a continuous story reaching from the first man down to the Exodus from Egypt, and possibly as far as his own time. Of course this is not wholly history by our standards, but within the limits of the material available to the Yahwist, it still reflects a remarkable sense of history. Here and there we can discern the words of the Yahwist himself, which are intended to interpret to us the material he has selected, and to enable us to follow the thread which formed for him the meaning of his narrative.

Now the quite distinctive feature of this pioneering venture into history writing is the way in which the Yahwist led his readers' attention away from the ancient practice of turning to the priests and cultic practices for discerning the will of the gods. The Yahwist turned the spotlight not on the sanctuary, but on the human scene of historical event, as the sphere in which the will of the God of Israel became manifest. This change in focal-point cannot be over-emphasized, for it is the key to much which happened later in the faith of Israel, and which is again happening in the new world to which Christendom has given birth.

This receives further emphasis when we turn to the second main corpus of historical material in the Old Testament. This consists of the books called Joshua, Judges, Samuel and Kings, which together form a consecutive history of Israel covering the period of the occupation of the Promised Land from the time of Joshua's entry until the Fall of Jerusalem in 586 B.C. Here, too, there are included many earlier blocks of material which have been pieced together, and these include the finest piece of historical narrative in the Old Testament. It is to be found in 2 Samuel 9–20 and 1 Kings 1–2. It is often referred to as the 'Succession Story' for it deals with the historical problem of who was to succeed David as king. It is judged by many scholars to have been written by one who had lived as an eye-witness through that critical period, and who gathered the necessary information together to write this account of that important crisis.

The historical problem with which this writer was dealing may be briefly described as follows. Before King David all of Israel's leaders had been of a charismatic kind, and were believed to have been raised up by God to meet particular crises. The personal prowess of the young David had led all the Israelite tribes finally to accept his rule and from that point he went on to establish a kingdom, and indeed a minor empire, such as Israel had not previously experienced. There had as yet been no dynastic rule. The approaching death of David therefore raised vital questions on which Israel's future existence depended. Was the day of charismatic leadership over? Would the kingdom of David disintegrate on his death? Could the stability of the kingdom be sustained by the establishment of dynastic rule? If so, which of the many sons by various wives should succeed him?

Thus the last years of David's rule witnessed the working out of these problems, and the consequent clash among several of David's sons for the throne soon to be vacant. Our unknown historian not only shows a penetrating knowledge of human nature in the way he sketches the characters of the piece, particularly David himself, but he soon makes the reader aware that his story is not a succession of meaningless events. The historian keeps his own sympathies out of the story, and makes no attempt to hold his characters up to praise or blame. Yet his narrative shows that each of the characters contributes to the complexity of the situation, in which ambition, guile, and secret plotting end in various acts of judgment. When, at last, Solomon is king and all rivals are vanquished, the history is brought to an end with the words, "So the Kingdom was established in the hand of Solomon."

Here we have no piece of theocratic history or myth, but a straightforward, and so far as we can judge, faithful account of a very human situation on which so much hung for the future of Israel. Eduard Meyer, a distinguished German historian of the turn of this century, described this historical writing as purely secular, and of it he said, "Thus the golden age of the Hebrew monarchy produced genuinely historical writing. No other civilization of the ancient East was able to do so. Even the Greeks achieved it only at the height of their development in the fifth century, and then as quickly fell away again . . ."

In this otherwise secular historical writing there are only three hints of a theological character. After the shameful incident between David and Bathsheba is concluded, there comes the comment, "But the thing that David had done displeased the Lord". When Solomon, the future successor to David, is born we read, "And the Lord loved him". At the crucial point in Absalom's rebellion against his father David, we are told that "the Lord had ordained to defeat the counsel of Ahithophel, so that the Lord might bring evil upon Absalom". Imperceptible though these hints may appear, the reader should remember them when he gets to the end of the story and recognize that the historian sees a purpose being worked out in the history he relates.

Gerhard von Rad, a renowned Old Testament scholar of our day, has shown how revolutionary was this view of history when it was first put forward. Up until this time the activities of the gods were expected primarily in natural events, particularly the miraculous and the extraordinary, such as earthquakes, storms and famine. But this historian believed that to the eye of faith the works of God were to be seen in everyday life, in events both public and private, and in secular affairs rather than in religious activities. "With this work," writes von Rad, "there begins a wholly new conception of the nature of God's activity in history."

We have looked at only two examples which illustrate how the Old Testament writers were concerned with history. They were two of the earliest but they were followed by many others. Israel was always trying to evaluate the present in the light of the past. To do this she was not afraid to reinterpret the past in the light of new events in her own day. Consequently the Old Testament contains not just *one* interpretation of history, but several, and each is related to the circumstances of the period which brought it to light. Among Israel's interpreters of history we must number the great prophets, for though, so far as we know, they did not themselves write any historical narratives, the divine oracles they proclaimed as coming from the mouth of God were all steeped in the historical sense of which we have been speaking. The prophets of the eighth and seventh centuries B.C. were the prophets of crisis, who interpreted to Israel the catastrophes in which first one, and then the other Israelite kingdom was swallowed up in the imperialist expansion of Assyria and Babylon respectively.

Thus in contrast with the ancient mythological cultures and with holy scripture outside the Judeo-Christian stream, most of the Old Testament either consists of historical material, or is expressed with due regard to the historical nature of human life. This led Israel to pay particular attention to what was going on in the world in her own day. National affairs and international affairs constituted the raw material for theological thought about the questions of human destiny. For Israel, God was to be sought both in nature and in history, but chiefly in the latter. He was for her the Lord of history. Modern Old Testament scholarship is continually emphasizing that Israel's theology, as expressed in the Old Testament, is essentially a theology of history.

This concern with history is continued in the New Testament, which records a further set of historical events of quite outstanding importance. The ministry of Jesus started with the proclamation, "The time is fulfilled, and the kingdom of God is at hand". An air of expectancy and of imminent cosmic change pervades the New Testament, even as the apostles go out to proclaim the events of the life, death and Resurrection of Jesus Christ. The early church believed that God had spoken and acted in history in their own day in a way which lit up all that had gone before.

So far, we have been at pains to describe how a concern with history came to the fore in Israel earlier than anywhere else, and found expression in the Bible. But this does not mean that there is a complete absence of mythology in the Bible. Indeed this should hardly be expected, for it was only by degrees that the concern with history developed. It is not the actual presence of mythological material in the Bible that is surprising, but the very small amount of it relative to the whole.

Almost the only element of pure mythology in the Old Testament is found in a few verses in Genesis 6, where it is reported that divine beings fell in love with human beings, married them, and gave rise to a hybrid race, presumably half-divine and half-human. There are several places where myths of the ancient world are clearly reflected, such as the story of the Garden of Eden, but these myths have been remoulded by the Yahwist and other writers to serve another purpose. They have been largely stripped of their original mythological elements, and have become rather like parables.

Generally speaking, the more the sense of history developed and turned Israel's attention to the human scene, the more the elements of ancient mythology were discarded. Yet there was always a cultural battle going on between the two, and the prophets may be regarded as the chief champions of the view that God is the Lord of history. It is probable that popular religion in Israel was much more mythological than the Old Testament, for the simple reason that the latter records the vanguard of Israel's thinking. Because each generation has, in a sense, to pass through all the stages of human evolution, both biologically and culturally, there is always a tendency for men to revert to mythology.

We are not surprised therefore to find that when, from the Exile onwards, the Jewish remnant of Israel was dispersed among foreign cultures which were still predominantly mythological, there was a resurgence of the mythological elements in Judaism. The Persian religion of Zoroastrianism was the strongest influence in this direction. It revived interest in angels, which now became a hierarchy of named heavenly beings, each with particular tasks to perform. It stimulated an interest in an after-life by contributing a doctrine of rewards and punishments in another life beyond the grave. The very term 'Paradise' is of Persian origin.

It is because of the resurgence of mythology in Judaism in the two or three centuries before Christ, and the continuing influence of Persian and other Eastern religions, that we find more elements of mythology in the New Testament than in the Old Testament. This is chiefly to be seen in the frequent reference to angels, the personification of the cosmic power of evil in Satan, the story of the Ascension, and the birth stories of Jesus, both of which are expressed in terms of traffic between heaven and earth. The earliest affirmations of the Resurrection of Christ are already tinged with mythology, but were quite restrained when compared with the Resurrection stories soon to develop, and by the second century the trends already present in the Biblical material had led to pure mythology, as in the Gospel of Peter.

The concern with history pioneered by Israel did not put an immediate end to mythology. On the contrary, when Christianity spread into the Gentile world of Greece and Rome, and later into the Teutonic world of Europe, there was a strong tendency for mythology to be baptized into the faith along with the new converts and to flourish under a Christian guise. It is open to debate whether popular Christianity in the Middle Ages was very greatly different in character from the popular religion of ancient Persia, except that the name of the Saviour was different. By that stage the scene of human history was no longer the focal point for Christian faith, for it had now been superseded by the heavenly scene, where all that was really vital for men was decided. One's destiny was in the hands of a whole heavenly company of angels and interceding saints.

The emergence of the new world, with its increasing secularization, has brought about the dissolution of the medieval Christian mythology. Orthodox Christians have often regarded this increasing wordly interest and this human emphasis on the here and now as a deplorable departure from the true spiritual path. But in actual fact this is the very direction in which Israel was stepping out in faith three thousand years ago. The abandonment of the other-worldly interests and the increasing concern with the historical processes in the world of here and now, far from being a sign of Christian apostasy, represent the recovery of some of the essentials of the Judeo-Christian heritage.

With the modern return of interest in the meaning of history, it has been common for some biblical scholars to recognize the important role that history plays in the Bible, but to limit the Christian's concern with history to those events to which the

Bible witnesses. These events have been referred to as 'Salvation's history', as if the hand of God is to be seen only in a selected number of events of the distant past. But this does not go far enough. The witness of the Old Testament is that Israel was always concerned with her contemporary history, and was prepared to reinterpret her past heritage in the light of what she witnessed in her own day.

The Bible, therefore, leads us to pay proper attention, not only to the significant events in the period of origins to which it gives first-hand witness, but also to the human scene of our own day. Concern with an other-worldly mythology can form a tranquillizing escape from the moral decisions and duties which involvement in the historical world forces upon us. The Bible leads us to see the problems of peace and war, of politics and economics, of race relations and poverty as the very areas where the God of the Christian heritage is speaking His word in history today. In the events in which we are caught up, in the problems that confront us, in the crises which hang over us, we are confronted by the God of our fathers. The decisions we make in our human situation is our response to God. In these decisions we are making history, and in this history we are encountering the Lord of history, and working out our own eternal destiny.

CHAPTER 10

The Concern with the Word and the End of the Gods

One of the universal characteristics of ancient mythology was its multiplicity of gods, goddesses and spirits. In sharp contrast with this polytheism, the Bible affirms that God is one. It was the lot of Israel to play the pioneering role which led to a convincing monotheism. There are only three great monotheistic religions in the world, Judaism, Christianity and Islam, and their monotheism is to be traced directly to that of ancient Israel.

Monotheism, like the sense of history, is something we too readily take for granted today, just because we ourselves are the product of a culture which has been based on it for so long. When, in a Western setting, a Christian believer and an atheist enter into discussion about the existence of God, it is common for them both to assume the unity of God. In doing so, they are both indebted to Israel, for whom the oneness of God was a consistent and unique declaration. It received classic expression in Deuteronomy 6:4, "Hear, O Israel: The LORD our God is one LORD". These are the opening words of what the Jew refers to as the Shema, and even by the time of Jesus, the Shema had become the nearest equivalent to a formal creed that the Jew attained.

In her earliest period, Israel was not yet ready to deny the reality of gods which other nations worshipped, but for her there was one God only. Gradually this belief, that God is one, led her to abandon the remnants of mythology she had inherited from her cultural ancestors. So the Psalmists spoke of the gods of the nations as idols, and unambiguously proclaimed that the LORD their God was quite unlike the gods of other peoples. This means that He was to be sharply distinguished from the gods of ancient man.

In some respects Isaiah 40–55, chapters which are commonly attributed to an unknown Israelite prophet of the Babylonian Exile, may be regarded as the highest peak of Israelite thought about God. This prophet poked fun at the gods of the nations with fearless scorn, on the grounds that they were helpless and unsubstantial. In fact there was just nothing to them at all. In his chapters we find no reference to angels or any other supernatural power. On the contrary, this prophet was so intent on attributing all power to the LORD, that he put these words into His mouth:

> I am the LORD, and there is no other.
> I form light and create darkness,
> I make weal and create woe,
> I am the LORD, who do all these things.

But how did this faith in the one God arise? Was this divine LORD of Israel simply one of the ancient gods, who was now raised to such supremacy in the minds of the Israelites that all other rival gods gradually lost their effective reality? While there is some element of truth in this, it is only so because Israel herself necessarily reflected in her earliest period the traits of the mythological origins from which she emerged. The LORD was in the early stages described as if He were the storm-god, or even the war-god, but these are but the remnants of ancient mythology. It is important to discern the unique elements in Israel's faith which came steadily to the fore.

The first sign of uniqueness is in the proper name by which the God of Israel was known. This holy name has been preserved only in its consonants, YHWH, but modern Old Testament scholars believe that it was originally pronounced Yahweh. (The name 'Jehovah' is an incorrect version of the same name. It was first used in the sixteenth century, and derives from a misunderstanding of the Hebrew text.) By the time of Jesus the word was no longer pronounced for fear of breaking the third commandment, and God was referred to as 'the LORD'.

We do not know where this name YHWH originated. There are even two conflicting traditions in the Old Testament itself, one of which says that as far back as the time of Adam's grandson "men began to call upon the name of YHWH". The other, and more dominant tradition, however, asserts that the name YHWH was known only from the Exodus, and that it was revealed to Moses by YHWH Himself. It is not possible to separate history from legend in the Exodus tradition, and so we cannot say just what actually happened.

But the important emphasis of the tradition is that YHWH was associated for Israel, not with mythology, as were the gods of ancient man, but with the events of her own history. The ancient gods derived their meaning and role from the phenomena of nature, but Israel explained their introduction to the name YHWH, and the import that this holy name had for them, in terms of the historical context in which she originated as a people. This is clearly seen in the introduction to the Decalogue, "I am YHWH your God, who brought you out of the land of Egypt, out of the house of bondage". For Israel, YHWH was the 'out-of-Egypt-bringing God'. When the Old Testament speaks about God, it is not referring to one of the many gods which derived from the imagination of ancient man, but to the one and only YHWH, who not only brought them into being, but also continued to be the Lord of history.

The Israelite affirmation that YHWH is the one and only God has important implications. Since YHWH is one, and since He is God, then everything in human experience and understanding stands in relationship to Him. He is not only the Lord of history, but also Creator of the universe. He is the source of truth, and for this Israel used a word which came from the Hebrew root *Amen*. This word describes that which gives firm support, that which is the pillar or ground of whatever has some degree of permanence. No wonder Israel called YHWH the God of Amen. This basic word supplies a whole family of words so essential for Israel's faith, which we translate as 'truth', 'faithfulness', 'faith', 'believe', 'trust'.

All truth, all sound learning, all reliable knowledge stem ultimately from God. Everything that happens in the world of nature, everything to be observed in human experience finds in Him its unity. If God is one, and is not at cross-purposes with Himself, then the inconsistencies in life are only apparent and are due to man's limited understanding. Forces and phenomena which appear to be quite unrelated are in fact related, for they emanate from God in whom there is neither division nor conflict.

These implications of the unity of God were destined eventually to supply the seedbed for modern science. It is being acknowledged more and more these days by historians, scientists and theologians that modern science not only in fact did take its rise within Christian culture, but could not have developed without the presuppositions which it supplied. C. F. von Weizsäcker (1912–), an eminent physicist and philosopher, said in his Gifford Lectures; "the concept of exact mathematical laws of nature which was only dimly present in Greek thought gained far greater convincing power by means of the Christian concept of creation. Thus I think it is a gift of Christianity to the modern mind." It is out of the vigorous affirmation of the unity of God the Creator that men were led to postulate and seek basic laws to which all natural phenomena conform.

A further implication of the unity of God is seen in the absoluteness of moral values. In a polytheistic setting it is possible to play one divine spirit off against another, and thus escape the demands made by moral issues. In the medieval Christian mythology, for example, the saints, the Virgin Mary, and even Christ were appealed to by the believer as a way of escaping the demands of justice associated with God. But when the oneness of God is paramount this is impossible, for it is God alone with whom one has to deal. Before the one God there can be no evasion of our human responsibility. His Word is absolute and final.

Moreover, the faith that YHWH was the Lord of history meant that in contrast with the mythological cultures, where the gods were little interested in human affairs, the spotlight of divine concern was pointed directly to the human scene. Nowhere else in the ancient world were moral demands brought so vigorously to the fore as in Israel. The prophets were the mouthpiece of YHWH in the concern for social justice and humanitarianism, and pioneered the way for all subsequent social reform. This all flowed from their concern with YHWH the one God and Lord of history.

But now we must ask in what ways Israel conceived of YHWH, if on the one hand He was acclaimed as their God and, on the other hand, He was clearly distinguished from all the mythological beings who had been referred to as gods hitherto. When we put the Old Testament material in its chronological order and make a comparative study of the way in which YHWH was understood and talked about, we get a fairly clear impression that Israel was steadily shedding the mythological elements from her thinking. In the earliest material God was pictured in human form, and described as if he made personal appearances in the human scene from time to time. The material from the next stage avoided these theophanies, as we now call them, and spoke of an angel or messenger (the one Hebrew word has both meanings) as the means by which YHWH communicated with men. Later again, even angel-talk was avoided, and it was thought sufficient for YHWH to speak His word, and man heard it through the voice of a prophet, or in his own inner ear.

Israel became increasingly reluctant to offer any descriptions of YHWH, except in such elusive terms as the 'glory', 'light' and 'brightness' of His presence. Nowhere is this clearer than in the second commandment, "You shall not make for yourself a graven image, or any likeness of anything that is in the heaven above, or that is in the earth beneath, or that is in the water under the earth." The reason for this is that whatever these forms portrayed, it would not be a likeness of YHWH, and any adoration of it would therefore be idolatry. The implication is that there is nothing known in the whole universe, not even in the spiritual realm of heaven above, which can be taken to be a true likeness of YHWH.

The implications of Israel's understanding of YHWH, as expressed in the first two commandments, are completely at variance with the way ancient man thought of the gods, and explain the iconoclasm which has been prominent from time to time in both Judaism and Christianity. Indeed both Jews and Christians have, on occasions, been labelled atheists, since they rejected all other gods and refrained from portraying their own God YHWH in any of the forms that ancient man associated with the gods.

It is but a logical step further to conclude that if the God of Israel cannot be likened to anything that is known or seen by man, then neither can He be adequately portrayed in the forms of language. Neither a mental image, nor a verbal image are any more successful in portraying the God of Israel than a graven image or painted picture. This means that the God of the Israelite heritage defies definition. Israel and her Jewish successors refrained from allowing any form of words about God Himself to harden into an absolute doctrine. They were concerned with that action which was obedience to YHWH, rather than with right understanding of the being of YHWH. They were ready to recognize that the God whose word they heard in their history, must forever remain beyond man's comprehension. He is the God of faith and not the God of knowledge.

This is a most important difference. When ancient man expressed his gods in visible form and gave them names, he was taking the first steps towards gaining the mastery of them. The possession of expert knowledge of the gods meant that the human worshipper knew just how to approach them in supplication and ritual and win their favour in order to achieve his own ends. Knowledge of the gods meant that man had the gods just where he wanted them. Man is always seeking this kind of absolute control over his world. But Israel recognized that YHWH can never be known in this way, for He does not come within the scope of those certainties which man can master with his mind and so manipulate for his own ends.

Christians, for the most part, continued the Israelite ban on the portrayal of God in visible form, though it did become one of the differences which finally caused the Eastern and Western churches to break from each other in 1054. But because the early church inherited from Hellenistic culture the love of penetrating into the truth by intellectual enquiry, the Christian thinkers of the West have too commonly concluded that they could define and delineate the being of God in the forms of human language with some confidence. Both Catholic and Protestant have often attributed to formal doctrines about God a finality they cannot bear.

For Christians, admittedly, the question was made more difficult by the claim that God had chosen to reveal Himself in Jesus Christ. But it must be remembered that the Christ of faith is no more visible to the Christian believer than God is. The New Testament writings can in no sense capture or limit the Christ, who is the risen Head of the Church, for He can be apprehended by faith alone.

John, the New Testament writer who most clearly claims that when one sees Jesus one sees the Father, is also the one who twice declares that 'no man has ever seen God'. This reflects the penetrating Old Testament story in which Moses asked to see the glory of God. He was placed in a cleft in the rock, and the hand of God covered the eyes of Moses so that he saw only the back of God. In other words, Israel recognized that one can see only where God has been; no man can see the face of God and live.

In the new world, much of what orthodox Christianity has assumed to be the sure knowledge of God seems to have dissolved away leaving the Christian with a certain sense of loss. He need not be bewildered. There are good biblical reasons why this should have happened. The YHWH of Israel, who was also the God and Father of Jesus Christ, does not belong to the ancient order of supernatural beings who can be neatly described by man's carefully chosen words. It is a mistake to think that Israel was slowly groping after the true God, who then finally answered them by coming down and showing Himself. This is the very kind of mythology from which Israel was being delivered by the word of YHWH. Israel testifies that YHWH is completely other than such gods. He defies description and definition, and is known only through His actions in human history. In Israel's experience He became more and more hidden from the human eye rather than less. It is at the peak of Old Testament thought that the prophet declares, "Truly, thou art a God who hidest thyself, O God of Israel, the Saviour."

But while Israel increasingly acknowledged that their God YHWH could be neither seen, described, nor intellectually mastered by men, she was on the other hand adamant in affirming that God was not silent. YHWH was known through His word. God spoke through the prophets, making them His human mouthpiece, so that the oracles they uttered were in the first person, as if God had taken temporary possession of their mind and body. God spoke to Moses from a burning bush and called him to lead Israel out of slavery. God spoke to Abraham and said, "Go from your country . . ." God spoke to the first man and said to him in his hiding-place, "Where are you?" Indeed, it was by the Word of

God that the world was created, for God had only to say, "Let there be light!" and there was light. Such was the unmistakable testimony of Israel.

The theme continued in the New Testament, where an unknown writer says, "In many and various ways God spoke of old to our fathers by the prophets; but in these last days he has spoken to us by a Son". John, in his Gospel, takes up the theme, interpreting the whole testimony of Israel concerning God in terms of the Word, "In the beginning was the Word, and the Word was with God, and the Word was God". And then he strikingly interprets the significance of Jesus of Nazareth by saying, "And the Word became flesh and dwelt among us, full of grace and truth".

In turning men away from the mythological concepts of the gods, to the YHWH who was known through His Word, Israel seized upon the most important phenomenon in the human scene to become the metaphor for faith. The evolution of man and the development of language went hand in hand. Our very humanness is dependent upon the language by which we communicate and grow to some degree of human maturity. With the development of each individual, language is drawn out of him by his elders who speak to him. So the very deepest insights about human existence that came to her, Israel described as the Word of YHWH. It was addressed to her from without, even though it was heard from within. As Israel learned, in obedience to the Word of YHWH, to shed one by one the mythological concepts of the ancient gods, it was the Word that remained. There was much she could not understand and never would be able to understand, but of one thing she was sure. She had heard the Word of YHWH, speaking now in promise, and now in judgment, but always summoning to decision and action, and she had no choice but to obey.

The fact that Christian thought has sometimes been tempted to revert to a doctrine of God more mythological in character than that of Israel, should not hide from us the direction in which the testimony of Israel was heading. YHWH was Israel's name for the one reality with whom all men have to do, and this one reality can never be mastered by man like the gods of the nations. In fact YHWH spells the end of all the gods and mental images which men create to bring themselves comfort and security. YHWH the God of Israel is always beyond man's grasp, and can be contained neither in temples, nor in pictures, nor in words. He can be spoken of, referred to and obeyed, only because in the events of daily life and history men have found themselves addressed by Him. It was the greatest prophet of Israel who wrote, "the word of our God will stand for ever".

CHAPTER 11

The Concern with the Earth and the End of Heaven

Israel's concern with human history caused her to fasten her attention more and more on the tangible world, the earth, and less and less on the unseen world called heaven. The abolition of the gods was destined to entail the abolition of the unseen world in which ancient man supposed them to live. The myths of ancient man were predominantly concerned with descriptive narratives of what went on in that divine world hidden from human sight. The Old Testament almost completely lacks this mythological interest, one of the few examples being the prologue of the book of Job, and this is very likely an ancient myth which a post-exilic writer adapted to provide the setting for his magnificent poem on the riddle of human destiny.

When the Old Testament begins its main theme, which is the story of Israel, we find that God's promise is expressed in quite worldly or materialistic terms. God promised to Abraham a numerous posterity, and the possession of the land of Canaan. "I will make of you a great nation . . . To your descendants I will give this land". This theme continues through the stories of the patriarchs and forms the prologue for the much more important and rather more historically based tradition, of the deliverance from Egyptian slavery and the entry into the land of promise.

As the story of Israel proceeds thereafter the material becomes more and more historical. But though this story of Israel is set in the real world of human history, and becomes what we today would call both political and secular, it is for Israel the very ground of her theology. The story of how Israelite tribes established firm possession of Canaan, drove out enemy raiders, and met the very severe crisis of the Philistine invasion by the institution of kingship, is narrated in the context of Israel's encounter with YHWH. Political leadership, military defence, the establishment of dynastic rule, become the chief concerns of Israel's traditions, and are expressed as the chief concern of YHWH her God.

At the point where Israel recognized that YHWH must also be the creator of the tangible world, the Old Testament expressed this in a positive, world-affirming attitude. "God saw everything that he had made, and behold, it was very good." The psalmists proclaim that in the night-sky one can behold the very handiwork of God, and it makes manifest His glory. It is He, who has provided the mountains with strength, and who can still the roaring of the sea. It is He, who provides for the watering of the earth, that it may bring forth grain and food for the creatures He has placed upon it. The earth in fact, along with all that it contains, is YHWH's *magnum opus*, and it is His chief delight to be concerned with what goes on in it. What a contrast this is with the comparative lack of interest which the gods of ancient man were believed to show in the tangible world.

Israel's concern to affirm the essential goodness of the human world that God had made, did not prevent her from seeing the wickedness, evil, crime and tragedy that it also contained. On the contrary it led her to be caught up in the process of rooting out those evils, for it became clear to her that YHWH was not abandoning the world He had made, but was determined to achieve its renewal. Israel pioneered the movement for social reform and the renewal of human culture. Wherever the people of God in subsequent centuries have neglected this, they have deviated from the biblical tradition which Israel founded, in obedience to Him who has the earth as His chief concern. The prophets of Israel, if transported to the twentieth century, might have found themselves more at home in a political meeting than in an ecclesiastical council.

The prophets of Israel were the forerunners of the political reformers in the new world. They saw that their world was under judgment, not because people had neglected their tithes, their sacrifices and their temple worship, but because they had trampled on the poor, traded dishonestly, and showed neither mercy nor justice to the weaker members of society. One of their chief concerns therefore was with the widow, the orphan and the resident alien, the very individuals who had been deprived of their natural protectors.

The prophets never for one moment suggested any attempt to escape from the wicked world. They did not proclaim any comforting message that all would be well in the sweet by-and-by in a spiritual heaven beyond death. But they did hold out the promise that the earth itself would be renewed, and they looked forward to the time when a transformed human society would live in harmony. Among their poetic prophecies we read:

> and they shall beat their swords into plowshares,
> and their spears into pruning hooks;

nation shall not lift up sword against nation,
neither shall they learn war any more;
but they shall sit every man under his vine and under
his fig tree,
and none shall make them afraid.

Israel testifies to us in the Old Testament that the promises she heard from YHWH were earth-centred, and the blessings received from YHWH were to be found in the length and quality of human life. Since the study of the Bible was revived at the Reformation, the sheer earthliness of the Israelite hope has often been a puzzle to the Christian reader. Modern Christians have been inclined to dismiss the Old Testament as primitive, limited and unsatisfying. This is because we have inherited from the Middle Ages a Christianity that was world-denying and which insisted on directing men's attention away from this temporal world to an eternal home in a supernatural heaven above. But this medieval Christian emphasis constituted a resurgence of the very same mythological unseen world which Israel had earlier abandoned.

Christians have often searched the Old Testament for evidence of the orthodox other-worldly Christian hope. They usually conclude that the Old Testament contains no clear doctrine of a life after death, but they interpret this as meaning that Israel in her earthly-centred life had only reached the stage of beginning to feel after that eternal world above, the door of which Jesus is said to have opened to all believers. But this is to ignore the fact that in at least some of the ancient mythologies, the human search for immortality in the unseen world of the gods was one of the favourite themes. It was not because ancient man had never entertained any such hopes of immortality that Israel focussed her attention upon the earth, but because Israel deliberately turned her back on such hopes, as she cast off the mythological outlook to which they properly belong. This might be how ancient man saw his eternal destiny, but this was not how YHWH had spoken His Word to Israel.

The story of the Garden of Eden illustrates this emancipation from the immortality theme in a rather interesting way. Close study of this material suggests that the prototype of this story was originally a myth derived from Israel's ancestors. Indeed it appears to have been a story of how to obtain immortality by eating from the tree of life which enabled one to live for ever. But in Genesis 3 this tree of life is referred to only in two verses (22 and 24) which can be shown to be an intrusion into the present text, partly because they break the continuity, and partly because one of these verses breaks off in the middle of a sentence. If, as seems likely, these two verses have found their way back into the story from an earlier version that had been discarded, it illustrates how man, even when emancipated from the mythological, is always being tempted to restore it.

Now let us see what the Israelite thinker has done with this myth. He has deliberately turned round the story to be firstly a magnificent study of disobedience and guilt in the human scene, and secondly, though more subtly, to warn his readers against the search for immortality. He removed all mention of the tree of life, and made the tree of knowing good and evil the forbidden tree. The idea that it is within man's grasp to become like the gods (and so attain immortality) is now set in the mouth of the wily serpent as the very temptation most likely to lead the woman astray. The fruit that can do this is too good to be missed and the woman and her husband succumb. One of the several morals conveyed in this version of the story is that man is not intended to share the immortality of the gods, and the attempt by man to grasp it for himself lies at the root of his fallen nature.

In contrast with many others of the ancient world, Israel recognized the full implications of man's mortal nature. Man is made from the dust of the earth, and to the dust his body returns. Israel understood the destiny of man as something to be expressed within the context of the tangible world of earth, and within the limits which mortal existence places upon it. YHWH was the One who spoke to her within the historical context, who sustained Israel as a people from generation to generation, and who walked with the individual Israelite from the cradle to the grave. Such a faith led the psalmist to say:

> YHWH, thou hast been our dwelling place in all
> generations . . .
> Thou turnest man back to the dust,
> and sayest, "Turn back, O children of men!" . . .
> Thou dost sweep men away; they are like a dream,
> like grass which is renewed in the morning:
> in the morning it flourishes and is renewed;
> in the evening it fades and withers. . . .
> So teach us to number our days
> that we may get a heart of wisdom.
> Satisfy us in the morning with thy steadfast love,
> that we may rejoice and be glad all our days.

There were many times when the Israelite was deeply conscious of the moral problems, the frustrations, and the anguish in which his human mortal lot involved him. But for the most part he learned, in obedience to the Word of YHWH, to accept himself as a creature, who was earthly and earth-bound, and yet the recipient of more blessings from God than he deserved. So out of the context of his mortal historical existence he could pour out his praises to God with joy and gladness.

Israel's almost exclusive concern with the earth meant that, for her, the mythological heaven of ancient man was all but eliminated. There are many places in the Old Testament where 'heaven' is used to describe the dwelling-place of God e.g. "Hear thou from heaven thy dwelling place; and when thou hearest forgive". This is an understandable survival of the earlier mythology in which the sky above, with its fascinating heavenly bodies, to some extent visible yet always beyond the reach of man, was regarded as the domain of the gods. Yet though Israel accepted the usage of speaking of heaven as the dwelling-place of God, she could not tolerate the idea of confining God to such an area. The very prayer we have just quoted, also says, "Behold, heaven and the highest heaven cannot contain thee; how much less this house which I have built".

But that was the limit of Israel's interest with heaven. The idea that it is a realm where the faithful departed live in immortal bliss is quite foreign to the Old Testament. The only two humans of whom the Old Testament speaks as being in heaven are Enoch and Elijah, and according to the tradition neither of these men had ever died. Enoch is a mythical character from Israel's prehistoric traditions, and of him the Old Testament simply says, "Enoch walked with God; and he was not, for God took him."

Elijah, on the other hand, was an historical character, but the stories of him preserved in the Old Testament are strongly legendary. He was so full of vitality, and seems to have been so much of a mystery man, who appeared on the scene like lightning and disappeared again as quickly, that it was hard to think of such a man as ever succumbing to death. So we are told that he was taken up to heaven in a whirlwind on a chariot of fire, drawn by horses of fire. Israel retained her interest in Elijah, not because he had attained immortality on the other side of death, but because she believed him, having never died, to be living in heaven with God for an indefinite period, whence at any time he might return.

It was in the post-exilic period, after most of the Old Testament was written, that we see the rise of certain themes and hopes which were destined to come to the fore in the New Testament. The Jewish remnant of Israel had achieved only a partial restoration of their former community life in the Holy Land. They were still scattered round the Eastern Mediterranean in what is called the Diaspora, and the holy city of Jerusalem was subjected to one foreign conqueror after another. This brought them under the influence of the mythological interests which had continued among other ancient peoples. And the increasing imperial oppression they experienced led them to a certain degree of despair concerning this world.

Yet this despair was directed not against the tangible world as such, but against the present age of the tangible world that they were then passing through. They began to set their hopes on the coming of a new age, and here they turned to the words of the earlier prophets who had looked forward to a renewed society. Out of the traditions associated with the earlier office of the kingship in Jerusalem, and stemming from the covenant establishing the dynasty of David, there began to emerge various messianic hopes that the new age would be ushered in by someone especially anointed for the purpose by YHWH the Lord of history.

It is important to note that their hopes did not involve the abandonment of the tangible world, but the abandonment of the present age, and its projected replacement by a new age or era, just as the antedeluvian era was thought to have been succeeded by the era after the Flood. The new age was described in more extravagant terms than those the earlier prophets had used, partly because the evil of the present generation, it was thought, could be rooted out only by a more cataclysmic change, and partly because of the influence of mythological terms drawn from the other cultures. By the time of the birth of Jesus, there was in Judaism a general air of expectancy. They looked forward to the new age. A messiah of some kind was awaited.

The early church believed that Jesus Christ had inaugurated the new age, and that it would very shortly be consummated in its fulness. They preserved the same terms as had been current in Judaism, namely, 'this age' and 'the age to come'. We have earlier seen that the same Greek word can be translated as either 'age' or 'world', and that is why this very term appears in the Nicene Creed as 'the life of the world to come'. The later Christian interpretation of this as an unseen supernatural world existing contemporaneously with the tangible world is quite a distortion of the New Testament hope, where 'the world to come' is definitely that which comes when the present age of the world has passed away. (Compare Matt. 12:32 in both A.V. and R.S.V.).

All this needs to be made clear, for the word 'heaven' appears a good deal more in the New Testament than in the Old Testament, and there is a strong tendency for readers to assume that it means there what later Christian orthodoxy meant by the term, namely, an eternal spiritual sphere above this world where the faithful departed live with God. It may come as a surprise to learn that in not one of the approximately 275 instances of the use of the words 'heaven' or 'heavenly' in the New Testament, does it mean the eternal home of the faithful departed. Often it just means the 'sky', sometimes it is a synonym for God, and in all the other cases it is used in one way or another to describe the dwelling-place of God, just as in the Old Testament. As such, it is the present storehouse for such future blessings as God may later bestow upon the faithful, and that is why we often hear of a reward or inheritance preserved in heaven until the time when it is to be granted.

The Ascension of the risen Jesus to heaven is a story parallel to that of the ascension of Elijah. The story was meant to explain why Jesus no longer appeared to the believers. Like Elijah of old, He has ascended to heaven for an indefinite period, but before long, so the early Christians believed, He would descend from heaven in the same manner as the apostles had seen Him go. Then there would be ushered in in its fulness that new age of which only a foretaste had been experienced to date.

The Revelation of John is quite unique in the New Testament in the emphasis given to the unseen heaven above, yet even here, what John was invited to see through the open door of heaven was a preview of the future events which were yet to take place on the earth. ("Come up hither, and I will show you what must take place after this.") John tells that he saw a new heaven and a new earth, for the first heaven (dwelling-place of God) and the first earth (the present dwelling-place of man) had passed away and the sea was no more. Then he saw the holy city, the new Jerusalem coming down out of heaven from God. It would replace the old Jerusalem recently sacked by the Romans. Thus, in spite of the visionary nature of these descriptions, it is still the tangible world that is being talked about, but renewed and transformed by the power of God. We must not miss the final and dramatic point. It is not a case of the faithful being saved from a lost world to spend eternity with God in a heaven above. It is a case of a lost world being transformed by God to such a degree that He himself abandons His heaven and comes to dwell among men.

It was only when the expected imminent end of the present age did not eventuate that the first century Christian hope found in the New Testament entered on the long path of transformation which was to reach its peak in the other-worldly unseen heaven of traditional Christian thought. There were many factors in this transformation, one of them being the influence of Persian religion to which we earlier referred. It had already influenced Judaism, and it further influenced Christianity with its clear-cut doctrine of the survival of man beyond death, to face a divine judgment which led directly to either heaven or hell. Once Christianity became permanently divorced from its Semitic origins in Judaism, and was proclaiming its Gospel in a pagan context where the ancient mythology was still very much of a reality, it was natural that the idea of the unseen divine world above should steadily become more dominant in Christian thought.

The emergence of the new world has brought about the dissolution of the mythological framework in which Christian faith had come traditionally to be expressed. Christians need have no alarm about this, for the other-worldly concern with a supernatural unseen heaven, which has dominated traditional Christianity, is really foreign to the witness of both the Old Testament and the New Testament. The way in which the new world has focussed man's attention on the tangible historical world of here and now is, in fact, a return to the very road on which our spiritual forebears of ancient Israel took the pioneering steps. It is He who was the YHWH of Israel and the God and Father of Jesus Christ, who has opened up this new world to men. It is He, who calls men to abandon the traditional concept of heaven and to concern themselves with the tangible historical world as the sphere of human destiny.

CHAPTER 12

The Concern with Man and the End of Religion

Religion is a difficult word to define. Christianity has been almost universally regarded as a religion, and its adherents have claimed it to be the true religion, yet notable theologians of this century have declared that Christianity is not really a religion at all. To minimize confusion we shall for this discussion define religion as a body of beliefs and practices in which man's attention is directed towards one or more divine beings in an unseen supernatural world, upon whom he believes his true welfare to depend, and from whom he seeks the help of spiritual forces to enable him to live successfully.

In the ancient world the whole of human life was embraced by religion. It was particularly vital at those times in which man sensed the mystery of life and growth, namely birth, puberty, marriage and death, the sowing of crops, the spring lambing, the building of a new home, the going forth to battle. It came to expression in the myths in which man tried to understand his mysterious world, and in the ritualistic practices by which he tried to secure divine aid. The mythological world of ancient man led of necessity to religion.

But we have seen that Israel pioneered a path which was destined to lead to the abandonment of mythology, of the gods, and of the divine unseen world in which they were believed to live. Since these are the very terms in which we have defined religion, it means that the heritage of Israel was destined to lead eventually to the eclipse of religion also.

The chief factor in this revolutionary move was the increasing attention devoted to the nature and role of man arising from Israel's concern with history. Whereas ancient man felt himself to be at the mercy of capricious forces seated beyond his control in an unseen world, Israel came to recognize that man himself has been given power and responsibility to act decisively, and that it is on his own moral decisions that his life and destiny largely depend.

There is a very significant difference between the ancient myths and the biblical stories, in the way man's role is described. Ancient man saw himself in a very inferior place. In the Babylonian creation myth, for example, man was created as a kind of after-thought in order to perform the menial tasks, which otherwise would have been part of the responsibilities laid as a judgment on the defeated rebel gods. But in the Old Testament man is regarded as the very crown of creation, entrusted with dominion over all other forms of life. The world was made for man, and it is his function to "be fruitful and multiply, and fill the earth and subdue it, and have dominion over . . . every living thing that moves upon the earth".

It was inevitable that this much more exalted view of man would be reflected sooner or later in Israel's attitude to traditional religion. At first the change was almost imperceptible. The chief ancient ritual of intercourse with the unseen world was sacrifice, and in her earliest traditions, sacrificial practices of some kind were assumed as a matter of course. In the very story in which YHWH delivered the promise to Abraham, we are told how Abraham responded by building an altar. In the earliest tradition of the Exodus, we learn that Moses was leading Israel out to the wilderness for the celebration of a sacrifice in a rendezvous with YHWH.

We have already seen, however, that the very same men of Israel who were responsible for developing a sense of history, were those who began to lead men's attention away from the sanctuary. In the great prophets this attitude to traditional religious practices grew more revolutionary and iconoclastic. At first, as in the case of Elijah, it was the abolition of foreign sacrifices that was called for, but a century later this attack was taken a stage further. Amos denied any real place to sacrifice at all in the heritage of Israel, even if it were offered in the name of YHWH. He interpreted the Word of YHWH as saying to Israel:

> I hate, I despise your feasts,
> and I take no delight in your solemn assemblies.
> Even though you offer me your burnt offerings and cereal offerings,
> I will not accept them,
> and the peace offerings of your fatted beasts
> I will not look upon.

Isaiah condemned the sacrifices of his day in even stronger terms.

> What to me is the multitude of your sacrifices? says the LORD;
> I have had enough of burnt offerings of rams
> and the fat of fed beasts;
> I do not delight in the blood of bulls,
> or of lambs, or of he-goats.

When you come to appear before me,
who requires of you this trampling of my courts?
Bring no more vain offerings;
incense is an abomination to me. . . .
Your new moons and your appointed feasts my soul hates;
they have become a burden to me,
I am weary of bearing them.

It is sometimes argued that the prophets were not seeking the abolition of the sacrifices, but only their reformation, so that they should become the expression of a true spirit of worship. That is how later Israelites, and then Christians, did most commonly interpret these words. But it hardly does justice to what the prophets actually said. A century later, Jeremiah, speaking in similar vein, specifically denied that there was any divine warrant at all for the sacrifices. "For in the day that I (YHWH) brought them out of the land of Egypt, I did not speak to your fathers or command them concerning burnt offerings and sacrifices."

In their scathing denunciation of sacrifices, the prophets sought to see them replaced by a concern for the daily life of man. They believed YHWH, the God of Israel, to be concerned, not with cultic offerings and ritual, but with moral integrity, justice and goodwill. Isaiah concluded his oracle with this plea.

Wash yourselves; make yourselves clean;
remove the evil of your doings from before my eyes;
cease to do evil, learn to do good;
seek justice, correct oppression;
defend the fatherless, plead for the widow.

In the book of Micah the contrast is set out quite clearly.

"With what shall I come before YHWH,
and bow myself before God on high?
Shall I come before him with burnt offerings,
with calves a year old?
Will YHWH be pleased with thousands of rams,
with ten thousands of rivers of oil?
Shall I give my first-born for my transgression,
the fruit of my body for the sin of my soul?"
He has showed you, O man, what is good;
and what does YHWH require of you
but to do justice, and to love kindness,
and to walk humbly with your God?

As a result of the teaching of the prophets there did take place a religious reformation, in which all the village altars were abolished and their sacrifices suspended. From that time onwards sacrifices were to be offered at one place only, the temple in Jerusalem. Yet even while the reformation was in progress Jeremiah saw that it did not go far enough. It was the reformation of man's moral and spiritual life that was required, not just a clean-up of ritualistic practices.

The prophetic distrust of religion was not confined to sacrifices. In most mythological cultures religious practices centred upon a holy building, which was either the house of the god, or else the appointed meeting-place between the gods and men. Israel inherited from her ancestors the tradition of a desert tabernacle or 'tent of meeting', which served this purpose in the nomadic setting. In the reign of Solomon this dwelling-place of God was given more permanent form in the erection of a relatively large and magnificent temple.

The prophets became as distrustful of the temple as they were of the sacrifices. Micah was the first to prophesy its destruction at the hands of YHWH himself, declaring that Jerusalem would be levelled to the ground, and the very hill on which the temple stood would become a forest slope. The clear implication is that YHWH was not concerned with holy buildings in the same way as were the gods of ancient man. At the very time when the temple was becoming an exclusive focal point of Israel's religion, Jeremiah saw that it was inducing in men a false sense of security. So he pointed to the well-known ruins of the earlier sanctuary of Shiloh as a sign that the Jerusalem temple too was destined for destruction, for the religious practices in it were leading Israel into a false faith, dishonesty and immorality.

Thus, in the very things most characteristic of the religion of ancient man, namely altars, sacrifices and temples, the prophets of Israel took the first steps in the direction of their abolition, for YHWH, being wholly different from the ancient gods, neither required the old cultic offerings, nor did He dwell in a house made by hands. The prophets turned Israel's attention away from the sanctuary to the daily life of man in society. Whereas ancient man attempted to bring some influence to bear upon the unseen world by taking his offerings to the holy place where he believed the gods to dwell, the prophets proclaimed that YHWH had come to man where he was. Whereas ancient man yearned for an immortal existence among the gods, the prophets declared that YHWH had chosen to dwell among men. Human affairs assumed a new dignity and eternal significance.

Both the sacrifices and the temple did come to a sudden end when Judah was overwhelmed by the Babylonians and the city of Jerusalem sacked in 586 B.C. The proclamation of the prophets was dramatically fulfilled. Even though some seventy years later the temple was rebuilt and sacrifices reinstated, this step proved retrogressive, leading to a period of stagnation. It came to an end when the final destruction of the temple by the Romans in A.D. 70 brought to fulfilment those words of an even greater prophet, "There will not be left here one stone upon another, that will not be thrown down".

But in the meantime the non-religious concerns of the earlier prophets had found new forms of expression in the emerging institution of the synagogue, which pioneered quite a new phase in man's spiritual pilgrimage. Here there was no altar, no sacrifices, no priest, and the building itself was not originally thought of as a holy dwelling-place of God. It took its name not from God, but from the people who gathered in it. ('Synagogue' is a Greek word which simply means 'coming together'.) In those days the synagogue would have appeared to a contemporary outsider, not as a religious place at all, but as a secular building, such as a school or a reading room. Some scholars have described it as a laymen's institute. It was primarily a place for those who had inherited the faith of Israel to gather for the study of the Holy Scripture which enshrined that faith. The written word of YHWH had now replaced the altar as the focal point of the community, and it was natural that their study of the Word should be in a context of the praise of YHWH and prayerful meditation. In our day the Jewish synagogue looks to us much like any other religious building, but in its original setting it must have looked decidedly secular.

It was because of the rise of the institution of the synagogue, that Jewish faith and culture not only survived the final destruction of the temple and the cessation of sacrifices, but even flourished. The Jews lamented the loss of the temple, but found, perhaps to their surprise, that they could get on without it. Yet even before it happened, Judaism gave birth to the new movement of Christianity, which owed more to the synagogue than it did to the temple.

In Jesus of Nazareth we find the true successor to the prophets of Israel, whose concern for the common man, and whose unconcern for the forms of ancient religion, He not only shared, but took to their logical conclusion. He was neither a priest nor a rabbi. He spent most of His life as a village carpenter. His actions and words are mainly recorded as taking shape by the seashore, on the open road, or in a friend's house.

Although a new religion eventually formed round His person,

there is little historical foundation for the assertion that He set out to found such a thing. The impression we receive from the gospels, particularly the earlier ones, is that the practices commonly regarded as religious by the ancient world are never more than incidental to what He had to say. The sayings gathered in the Sermon on the Mount, and in the parables of the Kingdom, show that like the earlier prophets He was chiefly concerned with the quality of a man's daily life. In contrast with the priest from the temple, and the scribe from the synagogue, Jesus was listened to gladly by the common people, and finally it was not the irreligious, but the religious authorities who had Jesus put to death, for He constituted too severe a threat to the vested interests of religion.

The early Christian movement spread first of all in the synagogue and derived its earliest forms and practices from it before being eventually cast out to live an independent existence. It was thrust more deeply into the common life of man, and further away from commonly accepted forms of religion. It had good news to proclaim about man's new freedom, and about the new world which would shortly replace the old one. It called men to a life of faith and obedience which transcended the religion of both Jew and Gentile, though it claimed to be the genuine consummation of the heritage of Israel.

For two centuries or more the Christians had no need of special buildings. It was not buildings that mattered but people. Those who professed the new faith became themselves the very dwelling-place of God through the indwelling risen Christ. The early church was the community of the faithful, and Paul transferred the word 'temple' to the human body as 'the temple of the holy spirit'. The Christians had neither sacrifices, nor holy temples nor priests. They gathered in one another's homes for fellowship meals, for the hearing of the Gospel, for the prayers and joyful songs in which they expressed their praise and gratitude to God for the newly received faith and hope. In contrast with ancient religion, the Christian Way (as it was called) was something new in human history.

It is roughly from the end of the first century, when the earliest Christian proclamations were already requiring some reinterpretation, that some aspects of the ancient character of religion began slowly to return. We see the climax of this process in the Middle Ages by which time Christianity had become a fully-fledged religion in the ancient meaning of the term. It focussed attention on holy places. It had developed a priesthood, and the original fellowship meal had been transformed into a sacrifice on an altar. It had become engrossed with an unseen supernatural world, where, by means of religious exercises, man was encouraged to secure a place for himself. It was a far cry from the concern of the prophets of Israel, of Jesus, and of the early church to see this world transformed by the coming of the new age.

The Renaissance and the Reformation reversed this long process which had led to the resurgence of ancient religion in a Christian dress, and they made way for the emergence of the new world with its renewed emphasis on the human scene. It is unfortunate that both Protestant and Catholic became so obsessed with the matters which divided them, that it was left more and more to laymen, as scientists, philosophers and historians, to take the adventurous steps in developing the new world. Catholic and Protestant ecclesiastics fell more and more into a conservative rear-guard role.

This has given the impression that the emergence of the new world, and the advent of the secular, have been initiated by those who had broken with the Christian tradition, and who have achieved success in the teeth of ecclesiastical opposition. There is some truth in this, but then, to men of their own time, the prophets of Israel and Jesus himself gave a similar impression. As we look back we can see that the Judeo-Christian heritage was making its significant advances through these men of old. We must learn to discern more clearly who the prophets of God really are in the new world. The fact that they may be holding up religion to judgment is no criterion for dismissing them, for at the heart of the biblical heritage we find a consistent movement away from the traditional forms of ancient religion to a concern with the daily life of man.

Much of what has appeared in the new secular world, and much of what has been said by the modern secular prophets finds its roots in the Judeo-Christian heritage. The new way pioneered by Israel and consummated by Jesus of Nazareth was not a new religion. It is essentially a way of faith, by which man, in whatever generation he lives, is summoned by the Word of God to concern himself with the human scene, for this is God's concern. Here he is called to grow to full manhood and contribute to the full potential of the new society. The Christian way transcends religion and spells the end of religion. It is not for nothing that we have been hearing in our day of religionless Christianity.

CHAPTER 13

The Concern with the Man Jesus and the End of an Age

The path pioneered by Israel, leading to the abolition of mythology, the gods, heaven and religion came to a consummation in the man Jesus of Nazareth, so that his coming spelled the end to the world of ancient man, and the new age in human history began, as is demonstrated by our division of time into B.C. and A.D. But before we can see this, we must let go our hold of that traditional picture of Jesus which Christian thought and devotion has built up over the centuries and which reached its climax in the Christian mythology of the Middle Ages. The new world has been effectively destroying Christian mythology, but the mythology surrounding the person of Jesus has been the last bulwark of orthodoxy.

The traditional picture of Jesus presents Him as a supernatural person from the unseen world, who deigned to appear in human form and spend some years on the earth among men. Because he was really God, he could perform all kinds of miracles, he possessed the knowledge of all truth, and every word he spoke remains true and absolute for all time. To show God's love and save men from damnation, he allowed himself to be put to death; but he knew that shortly afterwards, he would rise from the dead and ascend to his former home to sit at the right hand of God.

From the time the new world began to appear, men questioned this picture of Jesus more and more. But the New Testament appeared strongly to support it, particularly in the way it had been traditionally interpreted, and as long as the Bible could be regarded as an infallible source of truth, then that settled the matter. It was the new view of the Bible that finally shattered the traditional picture.

When a historian sets out to learn what a person from the past was really like, he looks first for records contemporary with the life of his subject. But for Jesus we have no relevant records written during his life, either by himself or by others. The historian then looks for records, which, though originating later, were written by men who knew the person firsthand. Here we draw our second blank. Though the memories of the disciples of Jesus are no doubt reflected in some way in the Gospels, it now seems probable that no New Testament book was actually written by one who had known Jesus in the flesh. The earliest New Testament books are the letters of Paul, and he gives no indication that he had ever met Jesus in the flesh, and he shows little interest in the earthly life of Jesus. The rest of the New Testament comes from the second and third generations of the Christian church, being written thirty-five years or more after the death of Jesus.

Last century this set many scholars busy searching the New Testament for the reliable human memories of Jesus it preserved, in order to reconstruct the historical picture of Jesus. There was a spate of books written on the life of Jesus. This inquiry received a sudden jolt when Albert Schweitzer wrote *The Quest of the Historical Jesus*, a book which showed, first of all, that the attempt to rediscover the historical Jesus had largely failed, and secondly, that the life of Jesus was set in a context largely foreign to us, this being marked by the expectation of the imminent end of the known world.

The search for the real historical Jesus had failed up to that date because each scholar selected and interpreted the Gospel material in a way which fitted his own presuppositions. But this is something which all Christians do in one way or another. When we read the New Testament we unconsciously construct in our imagination a picture of Jesus which is a rough and ready harmony of the four Gospels. We ignore, perhaps unknowingly, the inconvenient statements whieh conflict with our mental picture. The attractive figure of Jesus which each believer holds in his imagination must not be confused with the historical figure of Jesus, for it cannot even be reconciled with the New Testament, where there is not just one picture of Jesus, but several, all of which conflict at certain points.

This very thing that we find ourselves doing is exactly what the New Testament writers were already doing. What we have in the Gospels are not biographies of Jesus written by first-hand witnesses, but several portraits of the Christ of faith, written by men who had never seen Jesus in the flesh, and based on the church's experience of the risen Christ in their midst and on the memories of the earthly Jesus that had been handed down from the original disciples by word of mouth. We may still conclude that these portraits of the Christ of faith bear a reasonable likeness to a greater or less degree to the historical Jesus, but this becomes a matter of personal conviction. We are in no position to assert as an historical fact that Jesus did 'this' or said 'that' just because we read it in the

Gospels. The full and exact account of all that Jesus said and did during his earthly life is lost to us for ever.

In the New Testament we possess the early church's testimony to the Christ of faith, and their testimony, including even the remembered stories of Jesus, reflect at many points the church's own experience of the risen Christ they acclaimed their Lord. And after all it is not Jesus the teacher, nor Jesus the healer, who is at the heart of the Christian faith, but the Jesus Christ who is known by faith as the saviour and Lord of men. To this Christ of faith the New Testament does give firsthand witness.

When we ask what gave rise to the Christ of faith in the early church, we can immediately say that it derived from a certain complex of events in human history roughly centred round the year A.D. 30. Hardly anyone seriously doubts any more that there was a Galilean Jew named Jesus, who for a short time attracted local attention as a teacher who took an unusual interest in people and uttered some startling things, and who for this reason fell foul of the religious authorities, the result of it all being that the Roman governor had him crucified. This in itself is important, showing us how Israel's concern to see the meaning of human destiny in the scene of human history itself and not the unseen world of the gods, came to a consummation in the Christian faith. For the Christian heritage points to a human figure of history, Jesus of Nazareth, as the key to human destiny and the focal point of all to which history-centred Israel was leading. It proclaims that this event was of such a nature that the world was destined never to be the same again. (Those who want to interpret the advent of Jesus in terms of supernatural intervention are inadvertently attacking the most distinctive element in Christianity, namely its concern with history and not mythology.)

Secondly, the new view of the Bible has helped us to recover the true humanity of Jesus. This is not a loss, as some have thought, but a distinct gain, and constitutes a return to the distinctive witness of the Bible. In the ancient world there were gods in plenty who competed for the attention of men, but here was a man, a true man, who called for attention, and men found themselves giving him the attention and allegiance that they had previously given only to the gods. Israel had abandoned the gods of ancient man in favour of the YHWH who addressed them in history, and now in the Israelite human scene there appeared a man who not only spoke the Word of God but who embodied it in flesh and blood. This spelled the end to the gods of ancient man. The fact that the Jesus who became the basis of the Christ of faith was a true man in every way does not need to be argued away by

Christians, for in fact it is basic to the uniqueness of the Christian heritage. (This truth has traditionally been enshrined in the doctrine of the Incarnation, but so often the truth has been affirmed in one sentence and obliterated in the next by that quick flight back into mythology which has repeatedly been the church's undoing.)

The life of Jesus must be understood within the historical context in which he lived, and which helped to shape his thoughts and actions. It was an age of expectancy in which men, out of oppression and bewilderment, were looking hopefully for the new age to be ushered in cataclysmically by the anointed servant of YHWH. We do not know exactly what Jesus said about this and what he thought about himself in connection with it, but, whatever it was, the advent of Jesus led men to see in him the key to the new age, and their hopes suddenly blossomed forth with new vitality. Here was YHWH's man. Israel's concern for a renewed earth had arrived at a consummating point in the coming of the man Jesus, for through him the old world was now destined to pass away. The new age had come.

We have earlier noted how Jesus, in his ministry, took the questions of life out of the temple into the fields, the lakeside, the home and the street. There is no evidence that Jesus was greatly concerned with sacrifices, ceremonial purity, or religious exercises. The evidence rather points to his being concerned with the quality of the daily or secular life of man, as shown in honesty, integrity, and the readiness to give oneself in love to others. In the man Jesus the religion of ancient man came to an end. Thus the very things which we have seen to be both the distinctive elements of Israel's heritage and the seeds of the new world came to a sharp focal point in Jesus. That which was in Israel in the process of becoming had now actually arrived in the man Jesus. He initiated the new age.

But how did it happen? If Jesus was truly a man, why did he and not some other man give rise to the Christ of faith? There are no clear answers to these questions. But the simple fact remains that it happened. This is what the New Testament repeatedly affirms. A glorious and wonderful thing had happened. Something like a parable of this is expressed in the story of the man born blind. He could not tell how he had been healed or who the mystery healer was, but one thing he knew, "whereas I was blind, now I see".

We cannot even say at exactly what point of time the Christ of faith emerged from Jesus, that enigmatic man of history. Some have thought it originated in the ministry of Jesus, some have said it was on Easter day and some have pointed to the day of Pentecost as the birthday of Christian faith. But actually we do not know the history of that period clearly enough, as we lack contemporary records. We are not at all clear as to what happened between the death of Jesus and the conversion of Paul. Paul's letters are our earliest firsthand witness to the Christ of faith, but when he wrote them, he had been preaching the faith for some years.

Paul's letters, however, make it abundantly clear that for him Christian faith centred round the death of Jesus on the cross and the subsequent Resurrection. As an example of Paul's Gospel expressed in a nutshell, we may select Galatians 1 : 3–4. "Our Lord Jesus Christ, who gave himself for our sins to deliver us from the present evil age, according to the will of our God and Father." Here Paul reflects the current eschatological conviction that they were living at the end of an age—a wicked age that could end only in disaster on a cosmic scale. But it was the will of God that men should be delivered from that doomed age to enter into the new age. The self-giving of Jesus on the cross, in some way which Paul never makes clear, was thought by him to have achieved this deliverance, and this led him to "glory in the cross of the Lord Jesus Christ". The cross has always been the focal point of the Christian faith, and consequently it became the chief symbol of Christianity. Christian thinkers have been led to develop various theories of atonement which try to explain why the death of Jesus on the cross is so significant, but though these theories have a cogency in their own time, they never become permanently valid, for they are expressed in a framework of thought which belongs to the period of their origin.

When we ask how Paul came to be preaching the cross of Christ, then we find that his Gospel took its origin and shape out of his conversion experience on the road to Damascus. To appreciate the significance of that, we must remember that Paul was a Jewish scholar of no mean ability, who knew that in Israel's past, men like Abraham, Moses, Amos, Isaiah and Jeremiah had heard God speaking to them when they least expected it, and that they had been commissioned to tasks which had previously not entered their heads. Secondly, as a devout and passionately loyal Jew, Paul was intent on stamping out what appeared to be the smouldering remains of the cause begun by the now crucified Jesus.

In the short dramatic turn of events which halted him in his journey to fulfil this mission, he was temporarily blinded, and he heard a voice, which said, "I am Jesus whom you are persecuting". Paul found no way of evading the conclusion that the crucified Jesus was in some way still alive, as the Christians he was persecuting were then affirming. His own life was turned upside down, and he found himself commissioned to become an apostle of the death and Resurrection of Jesus. The new age he had awaited had burst in upon him.

Paul's experience is perhaps no better expressed than in his own words to the Galatians, "I have been crucified with Christ; it is no longer I who live, but Christ who lives in me; and the life I now live in the flesh I live by faith in the Son of God, who loved me and gave himself for me." Later he spoke of Christ being formed in those who heard the Gospel. Paul's conversion is the key to his faith and the Gospel he preached. The clearest evidence he had that the crucified and risen Christ was the Lord of the new age was in himself. He had become a new man, a new creation.

But Paul was not the first to proclaim as good news the death and Resurrection of Jesus, and he himself is our chief historical link with those who were. He tells us how he conferred with Peter, and James the brother of Jesus, and some years later with other apostles. No doubt they compared experiences. Paul was satisfied that they too had seen and heard the risen Jesus in experiences similar to his own. But if we seek further details of how they came to believe, and what it was they actually saw or heard, the answers are largely hidden from us. The historical evidence for the Resurrection of Jesus is to be found primarily in the apostles themselves.

The Gospel stories of the risen Christ, which have been highly valued in traditional Christianity through the centuries, are now regarded by New Testament scholars as containing many legendary elements, reflecting the developing traditions of the last quarter century from which they come. At the same time they genuinely reflect varied ways in which the crucified man Jesus made his impact upon them as the Christ of faith. Only believers testify to having seen the risen Christ, and sometimes they did not understand whom they had encountered until faith opened their eyes.

The New Testament nowhere describes the departure of Jesus from the tomb as a witnessed event in the way the later second century Gospel of Peter does. The nearest approach is in the story of the tomb found empty, which occurs in its earliest and simplest form in Mark 16: 1–8. The fact that Mark's version contains no supernatural elements, such as the later ones do, leads some scholars to regard it as having an historical foundation. But none of the apostles figure in this story, and whatever historical element may reside in it, it was not the finding of the empty tomb that brought the apostles to faith in the risen Christ, and if Paul ever heard the story he never thought it worth a mention, even when he assembled the evidence of witnesses in I Corinthians 15.

The resurrection of a man from the dead was not nearly such an extraordinary thing in the ancient world as in ours. The Bible refers to several instances. It is only in the late legendary material in the New Testament that the risen Christ is described in terms which imply that the Resurrection was simply the resuscitation of the dead body of Jesus. By that time various legends about Jesus were growing steadily, such as that of the Virgin Birth, and the more miraculous stories of what he did during his earthly ministry.

The Resurrection of Jesus must be understood within the eschatological context of the first century. There had already been a good deal of Resurrection talk before and during the life of Jesus. For in the hopes for the coming new age, it was expected that those who died before it arrived would be resurrected to take their place in it. Some even thought that the wicked would be resurrected too in order to receive their just punishment. Thus the Christian affirmation that God had raised Jesus from the dead was much more far-reaching than simply bringing the dead body of Jesus back into the tangible world. It was the triumphant declaration that the death of Jesus on the cross was not a miserable defeat, but the very victory which ushered in the new age. Jesus was not dead, but risen, the first-fruits of the great Resurrection which would accompany the imminent arrival of the new age.

There are three affirmations of the New Testament which must always be made in conjunction if they are to be properly understood, namely, the Crucifixion, the Resurrection and the new age. It is only because the Crucifixion led to the new age, that we can speak of the Resurrection. It is only because the crucified one is risen that we can speak of the new age. It is only because the Resurrection demonstrates the arrival of the new age, that we discern the significance of the Crucifixion.

But what of the new age? There is no doubt that in the days of Paul and the other apostles, it was expected very soon. Paul wrote, "For the Lord himself will descend from heaven with a cry of command, with the archangel's call, and with the sound of the trumpet of God. And the dead in Christ will rise first; then we who are alive, who are left, shall be caught up together with them in the clouds to meet the Lord in the air; and so we shall always be with the Lord".

But the years passed and the apostles died and the end did not come. Yet the Christian faith did not just die out. Slowly and almost imperceptibly, it adjusted itself to the new situation. It reinterpreted the New Testament conviction about the new age. What they experienced within the Christian community was evidence in plenty that there was a sense in which the new age had already come. That is why they were led to name the supposed birth year of Jesus as the point which marked the end of the old age and the beginning of the new. But they also knew that there was a sense in which the new age was not yet seen in its completeness. This formed the substance of the Christian hope and lay ahead in the unknown future. Eventually it came to be expressed almost exclusively in the mythological terms of a supernatural unseen world.

The mythological world of medieval Christendom has slowly disintegrated and out of the crumbling ruins the new world has emerged, and is still developing apace. It is only because of the medieval world that the new world has become a reality, and consequently the new world owes its being to the man Jesus just as much as the medieval world. Yet medieval Christendom had to die in order that the new world might appear.

Not everything in the new world is directly traceable to the man Jesus any more than everything in the medieval world was. The new world, however, bears unmistakable marks of the new age that he ushered in. But now, as then, the new age is both here and yet to come. The extent to which the future history of man will see the new age come more completely rather than witness a calamitous return to the old world, depends on the continuing recognition of where this new world came from. It derives from the historically-based, de-divinized, world-renewing, religionless heritage of Israel, which came to a focal point in the man Jesus. By his Crucifixion and Resurrection, the old world came to an end, and he ushered in the new age, an age which is still in the process of becoming.

CHAPTER 14

The Concern with Freedom and the End of Bondage

The Christian heritage has been commonly known as the Gospel, or Good News. It announces to men who are suffering under some form of bondage that the door to freedom has been opened up to them. Central as this is to the Judeo-Christian heritage, the particular form in which the Good News has been understood and experienced has varied considerably from one age to another. It is too often overlooked that it was the joyful message of deliverance from bondage which originated the Old Testament as it did the New Testament.

There is a clear dominant note running through Israel's written witness, whether in narrative, prophecy or psalms, and that is that Israel owed her very origin and her continued existence to a dramatic event in history, in which she was led out of slavery in Egypt to the freedom of a new land flowing with milk and honey. We have seen that YHWH, whom she called her God, was simply to be defined as the one who brought them out of the land of Egypt, out of the place of slavery.

Since our knowledge of this event is gained only from traditions which had been much embellished in the telling before being recorded in writing, we possess none of the historical details of the Hebrew slavery in Egypt. Its general historicity is confirmed mainly by the permanent mark it made on the national memory. Significant in the tradition are the simple words, "And the people of Israel groaned under their bondage and cried out for help". To whom did they cry? They did not know. When pressed to the limits of human endurance, one does not need to know before one cries out. Whether under the lash of an ancient Egyptian, or in the cotton fields of America, or in the concentration camps of Germany, it is often all one can do, simply to cry out, not knowing if the cry will ever be heard.

Their cry was heard. That is the triumphant and joyful proclamation of Israel. The Exodus saga tells how the angry young Moses made an unsuccessful attempt to help his fellow-Hebrews and then had to flee for his life. It was years later that he found himself confronted with an unexpected experience while pasturing his flock. From a desert bush, enveloped yet not consumed by fire, Moses heard a voice announcing that the cry of the Hebrews had been heard, and that he, Moses, was the one destined to lead them out of slavery to freedom. The voice was that of YHWH, and Israel's concern with the Word of YHWH dates from that time.

As the tradition is now enveloped in legend, there is no way of discovering the historical circumstances of the call of Moses, but we can be reasonably confident that there was such a man, who led a band of Hebrews in a dramatic escape from Egyptian slavery, and one of the oldest elements in the tradition is a song which celebrates the defeat of the Pharaoh's army in the waters of the Sea of Reeds.

> I will sing to YHWH, for he has triumphed gloriously;
> the horse and his rider he has thrown into the sea.

The deliverance from slavery not only gave the Hebrews freedom and a new lease of life. From this point onwards they became a new people, the people of Israel, whom the Exodus tradition actually refers to as the son of YHWH. There is good reason to believe that the Hebrews Moses led out of Egypt were only one portion of the people who later constituted the kingdom of Israel under David. But so full of vitality and promise was the faith engendered in them during the leadership of Moses that it soon penetrated the traditions and religion of all the people who lived in Canaan.

We have been accustomed to viewing Israel's early traditions through the narrow spectacles of the post-exilic Jews for whom religion had become a nationally exclusive affair. But in the kingdom of David there was quite a mixture of races. First of all there were the descendants of the various incoming Hebrew tribes, only some of whom had been involved in the Exodus from Egypt. Then there were the descendants of the Canaanites, and finally there were sprinklings of Hittites, Arameans, Philistines and possibly Ethiopians. We are even learning today that the very term 'hebrew' did not originate as an ethnic term, but as a term of reproach, like 'barbarian', which was given to various adventurous groups that had no settled abode. The kingdom of David, then, had a certain cosmopolitan character, and perhaps the ethnic diversity of the United States of America is the nearest parallel in the contemporary world.

Within this cosmopolitan Israel the sense of freedom, sparked off by the deliverance from Egypt and consummated in the kingdom of David, gave rise to a new kind of faith, which as we have seen, was destined to diverge more and more from the mythological religion of ancient man. This faith, even then, had a certain universal or catholic interest, a characteristic which was to blossom much more fully after the advent of Jesus. The Yahwist expressed the conviction that all the families of the earth would eventually be blessed by the faith which was beginning to flower in Israel and which he symbolized in the person of Abraham. Another example of Israel's wider interests was her concern for the resident alien within the community. "You shall not pervert the justice due to the resident alien . . . but you shall remember that you were a slave in Egypt and YHWH your God redeemed you from there."

It cannot be over-emphasized that the faith of Israel originated from a concern for freedom which arose out of a particular historical situation. This helps us to understand, even though it does not by itself explain, why the faith of Israel became concerned with history, the word of YHWH, the earth and the human situation, and why it progressively abandoned mythology, the gods, the unseen world and religion. But this concern for freedom in the scene of history did not remain limited to one particular event, which receded even further into the past. Israel relived the Exodus experience in her annual festivals, which became slowly transformed from the celebration of the changing seasons to historical commemorations of the events of her origin.

In the light of the Exodus tradition and its annual commemoration, Israel's thinkers were led to reinterpret the earlier tribal traditions and myths in such a way as to show how freedom from bondage is a basic human concern. The early Genesis stories clearly depict man as his own worst enemy because of the latent powers of self-destruction residing in him. The disobedience of Adam and Eve leads to Cain's murder of Abel, and this in turn to Lamech's vengeful inhumanity. The human race has within it the dreadful power to bring about its own self-destruction, and this is dramatically brought home by means of the legend of the great flood, where man was all but annihilated, because he had filled the earth with his violence and corruption.

The YHWH who led Israel from Egyptian slavery was identified with the one who had kept the door of hope open for humanity through Noah and his family. But no sooner had Noah become established again on dry land than he got himself drunk and the whole story of man's inability to control his self-destructiveness began all over again. The legend of the tower of Babel is effectively used to show that whereas language may be man's most distinctive characteristic, his own self-centred designs to make a god of himself result in a complete breakdown in that verbal communication upon which all human culture and healthy society depend. Words become a meaningless babble. Men become isolated from one another and are scattered in their loneliness.

In these few chapters which formed the preface for Israel's testimony to what YHWH had done in her history, Israel strikingly portrayed the spiritual poverty and bankruptcy of the human race. Man is in bondage to himself. He feels he has the potential for something which turns out to be beyond his reach. He becomes enmeshed in the chains of his own making. This is Israel's way of saying what Paul later so aptly expressed for every man. "I do not understand my own actions. For I do not do what I want, but I do the very thing I hate . . . Wretched man that I am! Who will deliver me from this body of death?"

Consequently, though Israel had been led from bondage to freedom, she found that freedom is a goal, rather than a possession which is finally won and possessed thereafter. Each generation, in the circumstances of its own time, seeks a deliverance from bondage, and is led to freedom only by obedience to the Word of YHWH. Without that obedience even such freedom as may still be a present possession, is lost in a reversion to slavery and destruction.

In the seventh century B.C., when first the Assyrian and then the Babylonian Empires threatened Israel's possession of their land of freedom, some men of Israel, whom we call the Deuteronomists, because their work has survived in the book of that name, saw that the crisis could be met only by returning to the Mosaic foundations of the faith. As they saw it, Israel's immediate destiny depended on a choice in which obedience would lead to freedom and disobedience to slavery, and this choice they set in the mouth of Moses. "See, I have set before you this day life and good, death and evil. If you obey the commandments of YHWH your God . . . then you shall live and multiply . . . But if your heart turns away, and you will not hear . . . I declare to you this day, that you shall perish . . . I have set before your life and death, blessing and curse; therefore choose life, that you and your descendants may live . . . that you may dwell in the land which YHWH swore to your fathers . . . to give them". The freedom to which YHWH leads his people may also be lost. That is the Word of judgment that YHWH speaks in history.

So the Jews were transported into Babylonian exile, and never again since that time have all the Jewish people lived in the land of Canaan. Once again they cried out for help, but this time there was a difference. The unknown prophet we have already mentioned, saw much more deeply into the real meaning of salvation from bondage. This prophet looked for the release of his people from forced exile and he hailed the Persian conqueror Cyrus, who actually made this possible, as YHWH's anointed king. But he also fastened on to the positive and redemptive meaning of suffering. In passages commonly known as the Servant Songs, he described the role of the true servant of YHWH. Whether as a people or as an individual he is one who accepts and bears suffering. Freedom is something much deeper than the deliverance from outward oppression, for man must be freed from the chains forged by his self-centredness and wilful disobedience. Deliverance of this kind is achieved only through suffering, and it is not for his own deliverance but for that of others that the servant of YHWH is voluntarily prepared to suffer.

In Job, Ecclesiastes and some of the Psalms, men of Israel wrestled with the problems of human existence. The traditional answers, as set forth for example by Job's three comforters, no longer brought satisfaction. There did not seem to be any clear purpose in life, particularly when it was marked by apparently undeserved suffering. In the three or four centuries before Christ there gradually developed a cultural maelstrom, and the Jews found themselves caught up in a clash of cultures, religions and imperialistic ambitions. Men became subject to a new and even worse form of bondage. They were enslaved to a meaningless existence. Even Judaism, which had itself descended from the Israelite faith which originated in a sense of joyful freedom, had for many Jews crystallized into a legalistic religion which constituted a new form of bondage.

Into the cultural maelstrom there stepped that enigmatic man Jesus, and out of the complex of events surrounding his advent there burst into the world a fresh, vigorous and joyful proclamation of good news. The unknown prophet's concern for vicarious suffering became a central historical event in the Crucifixion of Jesus. The cry for deliverance from a meaningless and doomed age had been answered by the very YHWH who had delivered Israel from slavery. The Gospel of Jesus Christ when proclaimed, brought to more and more men a sense of deliverance, a release from their burdens. It is by no means certain, and indeed not even likely, that all men who embraced the Christian faith were actually attracted to the Gospel for the same reason. Some Jews, for example, may have been attracted to Jesus in the first instance, because they saw in him the way in which the Davidic kingdom would be restored. There were others involved in particular personal problems for whom the preaching of the Gospel brought new vision and hope, and so it freed them from their burdens.

To the many who lived in dread of the imminent cosmic holocaust to which they saw the world heading, the Gospel brought the sense of being delivered to participate in the new age. For Paul certainly, and no doubt for other Jews, it brought deliverance from bondage to legalism, accompanied by a great sense of freedom. Such examples should be sufficient to show that the good news of deliverance from bondage, the theme which runs through the whole of the Bible, must not be interpreted in any one narrow sense. Whether the Christian Gospel was good news because it brought forgiveness of sins, deliverance from evil habits, or banishment of despair, depended on the particular circumstances in which it was being proclaimed. The Christian faith can be good news in all the variety of human situations, but to be so it will find many modes of expression. But fundamentally we may say that it is good news in all human situations because in one way or another it delivers man from some form of bondage and frees him for the fullest possible life.

Now it is one of the lessons of history that freedom is something each generation must seek afresh for itself. The freedom won by an earlier age so readily becomes transformed into a new form of bondage. The heritage of freedom handed down by ancient Israel became in Jewish legalism a new form of bondage. The glorious freedom in which the early church rejoiced had by the Middle Ages been transformed into a new form of bondage, actually the resurgence of an ancient form of bondage, that in which man was enslaved to his own mythological world. For medieval man the Christian Gospel meant the deliverance from the fires and pains of a future hell on the other side of death, and the assurance of a blissful eternity in heaven. (Those Christians who still hold such a view, have first to preach the fear of Hell into their hearers before they can then in turn preach the Gospel of salvation.)

The medieval Christian, in spite of his Gospel, found himself enslaved to an ecclesiastical system in which his future salvation depended on an intricate set of cultic practices. The very faith that promised deliverance had made him its prisoner. The Reformation was the first sign that this form of ecclesiastical bondage was destined to crack and give way to the emergence of a new world with a whole new concern for freedom. It is not surprising that it was through a study of Paul that Martin Luther, who had plagued his body in order to be sure of eternal salvation by the statutory methods of medieval religion, found a great burden fall from his shoulders, when he rediscovered the role of faith in bringing freedom to men.

But the Reformation of the church was only the beginning. In the last four centuries man's cry for freedom has been raised with increasing intensity and from diverse human situations. In successive political revolutions man has won civil freedom, throwing off the yoke of barons, kings, the gentry and now the wealthy. In the abolition of slavery man has sought freedom from the most ancient form of human bondage. In the emancipation of women, freedom is being won from subjection to the male. In the overthrow of imperialism each society seeks the freedom for independent self-rule. In the present racial clash man seeks to be free from the penalties imposed upon him because of the colour of his skin. In the new world technology is bringing freedom from drudgery, education offers freedom from ignorance, medical science is freeing men from disease, malnutrition and untimely death.

The concern with freedom which has come to the fore in the new world is that which originally brought forth the Word of YHWH, to which the Bible witnesses. The concern for freedom is basic to the Christian heritage, and insofar as the new world has brought to man a greater measure of freedom, it is to be recognized as the answer of the God of the Christian faith to the perennial cry of man. Wherever the new world has brought to man freedom from human domination, freedom from famine, freedom from physical or mental handicap, freedom for the fullest possible human life, the Christian finds grounds for great rejoicing. Where the signs of bondage remain, the Christian sees a task which the Word of God is calling him to share. For the world is still waiting to be freed from the fear of war and of a suicidal nuclear holocaust.

There is one thing yet more basic. With all the freedoms that the new world has brought and is still bringing, there has been developing another form of bondage. It is the bondage of the human spirit. The old cultural frameworks which gave scope to the human spirit are gradually being destroyed by the new secular world itself. That which is beginning to worry our age more than anything else is the fear that human life after all is a meaningless affair. It is clearly reflected today in art, literature and music. There is the fear that there is no purpose in history after all, and that the world is an impersonal cosmic machine in which the individual lives and dies, and vanishes into oblivion, so that it makes no difference at all that he has ever lived. For this reason even the freedoms that have been won may turn stale and tasteless in the hands that have received them. Man cries out in deeper anguish than ever to be delivered from the crushing burden of the sheer meaningless of human existence. The answer to this cry comes from Him who brought the new world into being, the YHWH of Israel and the God and Father of Jesus Christ. In the Christian heritage He still sets before men the choice of life or death. From those who respond in faith and obedience to His Word of life there still comes forth the joyful shout, "Hallelujah! For YHWH our God the all-powerful has come to reign".

PART III

The Meaning of Christian Faith Within the New World

CHAPTER 15

Faith as an Essential for Human Existence

Much of what has been traditionally regarded as orthodox Christianity has been progressively dissolved by the advent of the new world. The liberal extreme has been led to abandon Christianity as no longer tenable. The conservative extreme attempts to defend as many of the bulwarks of orthodoxy as it can, and for as long as it can. Each extreme results from a superficial understanding of the origin of the new world and the nature of the Christian faith, and the weakness of each constitutes a reason for the other's existence. By returning to the roots of the Judeo-Christian heritage, we have tried to show that the new world owes much of its strength to these roots. But if they are abandoned, the new world may cease to blossom and turn to decay, instead of bringing forth fruit.

To avert such a disaster, the Judeo-Christian heritage must be allowed to shed its outworn forms, and by finding that mode of expression most proper to the context of the new world, demonstrate to men that it possesses the same creative vitality that it has manifested in earlier periods. This is no time for clinging rigidly to the doctrinal formulae, the ecclesiastical systems and the liturgical forms of the past. We must learn to do without the security which such traditional institutions give us. Those committed to the Christian heritage are called quite simply to a venture of faith.

But what a paradoxical situation! Is not faith what Christianity is all about? While it has traditionally taken the form of a religion, and has appeared eternally committed to a large body of doctrine, Christianity has been most accurately described as 'the faith'. Jesus has been called 'the pioneer and perfecter of our faith'. The first Christian martyr was 'Stephen, a man full of faith'.

To learn how the God of the Christian heritage is addressing us in the new world, calling us, as he ever does, to venture into the unknown by faith alone, let us start at the very beginning and examine the nature of faith itself. First, we must look at faith in its most general form. One thing that should have come home to us from our study of biblical origins is that the Christian heritage is not a body of esoteric, supernatural knowledge which has been miraculously introduced into the human situation where it is somehow out of place. The Word which men heard from YHWH is that which came out of the historical scene. It addressed men through those elements which were already a part of the human situation, and faith is an essential for human existence.

What does it mean to have faith? Faith is an attitude of acceptance and trust. Christianity has no monopoly of it. Faith of some kind is as essential to the human spirit as blood is to the biochemistry of the body. Were there absolutely no faith present among men, there would be no community, and where a once strong community faith grows weak, civilization and culture give way to disorder and decay. The absence of faith in the individual is not so much doubt as distrust, isolation and utter loneliness. When a man has no faith at all, he is lost indeed, and it is from such that suicides result. It is far better to have an inadequate and superficial faith than no faith at all.

But there are different kinds and different levels of faith. A man may have faith in his car, in the Government, in his wife, in his pet theory and in God. In each case faith involves a relationship of trust which prompts the man to do certain things as a result. Indeed, it is only when faith does lead to decision and action that it manifests its reality, either to the man himself or to an observer. So the Bible says that faith without works is dead. The more faith one possesses, the more it leads to initiative, decision and action.

It is not just a part of a man, such as his intellect, which acts in faith, but the whole of man. Faith at its deepest and most all-embracing level is that attitude of acceptance, trust and initiative to which his total experience leads him. Faith is present in the human being from the point of birth, and it is in the infant that the intellectual content of faith is at its absolute minimum. Parentage and family setting provide the context which prompts and fosters faith from the human being's earliest experience. In the years of infancy and childhood parents provide the ground for faith, and are as god to the growing child.

It is only when the child has already been involved in a good deal of basic faith experience that he steadily attains more self-awareness, and his developing mind recognizes that the context of his human existence is one in which the horizons are being pushed ever farther back. Intellectual knowledge and beliefs, such as he has already absorbed from his cultural environment, now begin to play a larger part in the total body of experience which continues to nurture his faith. But faith is an essential ingredient of human existence at all levels. It is neither more real nor less real in the infant than it is in the intellectual genius, but in the maturer person there is much greater awareness of the grounds for faith and the challenge to commitment. The practice of infant baptism is the visible acknowledgement that from birth the child is being shaped by his faith environment; and the practice of confirmation of baptism is the recognition that on reaching years of discretion a person must decide for himself between commitment and rejection.

In every human community there is some degree of common faith, or else the community will fall apart and perhaps disintegrate. The vitality of a community and the strength of the mutual relationships of its members reflect the faith common to them all and the degree to which its members are actively committed to it. If there is to be active commitment, then there must be some degree of intellectual understanding of what the faith involves, and this in turn means that the faith is expressed in certain practices and doctrines. These forms give practical and verbal expression to the common faith of any one generation and, when handed on, become the vehicle for transmitting and nurturing the faith of the next generation.

But this can readily lead to the fallacy of identifying faith with the practices and doctrines in which it has expressed itself. In the case of Christianity, the fallacy has led many to think that to embrace the Christian faith one must give intellectual assent to a body of standard unchangeable doctrines which have been handed down, supposedly, from the beginning of Christianity. Unless one can accept, say, the doctrines of the Virgin Birth, the bodily Resurrection of Jesus, and the Trinity, then one cannot be a Christian believer.

But when we examine the history of any one of these doctrines we find that in their beginnings they were not the origin of faith at all, but the result or expression of it within a particular context. Let us take, for example, the doctrine of the Trinity. The word 'Trinity' did not even come into Christian use until about the beginning of the third century, and it was another two centuries before the orthodox form of it was hammered out in Christian thought. However much some may think the doctrine to be implicit in the New Testament, no one can maintain that it is explicitly stated there. To make Christian faith dependent upon accepting the doctrine of the Trinity leads to the absurdity that there were no fully Christian believers until the doctrine was clearly formulated.

Doctrines and formulated beliefs are neither to be identified with faith nor regarded as the origin of faith. Doctrines result from faith, and constitute the expression of faith for a limited historical period. Thus doctrines come and go. Sometimes what has been an orthodox doctrine for some long time has to be discarded. Sometimes a new doctrine comes to expression which has had no explicit forerunner at all. The history of the church illustrates this living, developing process over and over again. Too often Christians have clung to the doctrinal formulations of former generations long after they could be honestly held, and this has led to that all too popular idea of faith, so aptly defined by the schoolboy, as 'believing what you know ain't true'. Once a traditional doctrine ceases to be meaningful, it ceases to stimulate faith, and becomes a means of quelling faith. Many people in the new world have abandoned active commitment to the Christian heritage, not because they wanted to, but because the church led them to believe that the Christian faith was to be identified with certain dogmatic statements, which for them no longer had the ring of truth.

We must go behind doctrines and beliefs if we are to understand the origin and meaning of faith. Let us return to the family setting where the infant takes his first steps in faith. Leaving aside those infant actions which fall into the categories of reflex and instinct, we can discern the gradual appearance of responses which manifest the growing faith that the child is learning to have in his surroundings and particularly in his parents. These responses are not self-originated. Rather they are drawn out of the infant by aspects of the environment, particularly the care and interest shown by parents and the words they speak. Faith at its deepest level is personal, and is fostered in the newcomer to the faith-situation, by the faith that already exists in the community. It is widely recognized nowadays that the young child quickly learns to absorb the attitude of faith manifested by those around him, while, if such faith is deficient, the child too becomes diffident, perhaps distrustful, and builds up barriers in self-defence. Faith is an attitude to be experienced. It is not dependent upon prior knowledge, nor does it lead necessarily to knowledge of an objective kind. It is experienced most clearly in the human or personal situation, where there are so many unknown and unpredictable factors that the scientific method, which has been so fruitful in some fields, has shown itself to be quite limited in its application. It is not knowledge but faith which enables a person to blossom in maturity and wholeness. It is faith which creates the human community and makes it wholesome and stable.

If faith, simply as a human phenomenon, can do these things, then why is there any need to be concerned with some additional special kind of faith known as the Christian faith? First of all, it must be recognized that it is out of the heritage of Christian culture that we have been led to speak of faith in this general way, and to appreciate its role in the human situation. So widespread is the influence of the Christian faith in the culture that has nurtured us, that nothing we do or say is left uninfluenced by it. The second point is that it has been of the very essence of the Christian faith to have brought to light the role of faith in the human situation.

While this is by no means the sum-total of the Christian faith (as later chapters will make clear), it can certainly be said that the Christian heritage rests upon faith as the basic experience. The Christian heritage points to the way in which faith was drawn out of man by, what it calls, the word of God. The history of Israel as a people of faith begins with the story of Abraham, and of him the New Testament says, "By faith Abraham obeyed when he was called to go out to a place which he was to receive as an inheritance; and he went out, not knowing where he was to go." He received no map, no clear instructions, no guarantee of a safe return. He did not even have a signed affidavit which guaranteed that the voice he heard was the voice of God. But what he heard gave him faith; it gave him faith to hear it as the word of God, and he obeyed.

It is salutary for us to remember that Jesus is recorded as having recognized the presence of faith in the most unlikely places, even in those who had had no share in the inheritance of Israel. He did not ask men what doctrines they believed. He did not catechize them. It was sufficient to recognize in them the response of faith, and he said, "Your faith has made you whole." Just as the Word of God heard and proclaimed by the prophets of Israel engendered faith, so those who had known Jesus in the flesh had found him to be one whose very presence radiated faith and so brought forth from men the response appropriate to faith.

For faith, as we saw, cannot be separated from the action to which it leads. The man of faith is continually being prompted to actions and decisions, for faith which is engendered by the Word of God must lead to commitment to obey the Word of God. Yet it is not the clear and straightforward plan of action, that is most commonly associated with faith, but that which is begun with a certain amount of fear and trembling, and definitely with uncertainty. It is an act of faith just because it is not known for certain to be the right way. Abraham's journey into the unknown describes this very aptly. The path of suffering which Jesus chose to tread, the agony in Gethsemane, and the cry of dereliction from the cross, all reveal the intensity of faith, just by virtue of the uncertainty that marked each act of obedience.

In every generation the Word of God calls men to faith and obedience. In spite of all the accumulated Christian witness of the past, it must still be for the believer a path of faith and obedience. Men are continually tempted to evade this path by resting on the laurels of past generations. Appeal is made to the examples of the saints and theologians of the past. Admittedly they have much to offer us, but what they give must never be allowed to take the place of the road of faith into the unknown. Each person, on reaching maturity, must learn the path of faith for himself. He who seeks refuge in an infallible church or in an infallible Bible is less acquainted with the way of faith, than the person who knows neither of these, but who nevertheless obeys the word of God in the midst of his own uncertainty.

In the new world, God challenges men of all religions and men of none to go forward into the unknown in faith. Christians are not excused this challenge to faith just because they can point to the ancestral line by which they have inherited the Christian heritage, for the Christian heritage, when examined, is found to start with an act of faith. The Christian finds himself in the paradoxical situation that the more he thinks he knows about God and his world, the less justification there is for him to be called a believer, while the less he knows with certainty of God and human destiny, the more he is challenged to that obedient faith which alone can lead to wholeness of life.

CHAPTER 16

Myth as the Language of Faith

Faith is an experience into which a person is led by those for whom it is already a present reality. But for faith to be shared there must be communication, and this quickly entails verbal communication. Thus the experience of faith comes to be translated into a form of words. From now on we must discuss the verbal forms in which the faith of Christian believers has been most commonly expressed. As an example of the Christian understanding of faith in simple terms, we may take the words, "I believe in God through Jesus Christ our Lord and Saviour".

Now what sort of language is this affirmation of faith? Is it the same kind of language as that in which we say, "The battle of Hastings was fought in 1066" or "Water is composed of oxygen and hydrogen"? It is not! Actually it could be said that we have developed different languages for different purposes. For example, mathematics and biochemistry have developed languages of their own. So has human love. We have long realized that things can be communicated in poetry which cannot readily be expressed in prose. We should not be surprised if this most vital human experience called faith should have developed its own language.

Each language has its own rules and it leads only to confusion if we try to make one language conform to the rules of another. Human love has developed its own kind of verbal communication, but this language does not conform to the rules of logic. The language of faith does not become meaningless, as some critics of religious language are inclined to maintain, just because it does not conform to the canons proper to philosophy or history. But neither can the language of faith lead to conclusions which properly belong to the fields of history or philosophy.

Faith has developed its own language because it is attempting to express why man has been led to an attitude of trust, in the face of a human situation whose mystery is both impenetrable and tantalizing. Man finds himself with a stream of consciousness, which, in spite of all that psychology and neurology tell him, is a wonderful and inexplicable phenomenon. He has an imagination in which he may oscillate from seeing himself as but a speck in an unfathomable universe, to the other extreme of beholding the whole universe in his mind's eye. Why does he find himself called to respond to this human situation in faith? This question defies a conclusive answer in the language of logic. Not even good prose can adequately explain his reasons for faith. Like the poet and the artist, the man of faith reaches out for a medium of communication which transcends the languages which are adequate for discussing more limited areas of experience. The language of faith has more in common with poetry than with philosophy or a science. (Even for ancient man, poetry was regarded as the language of the gods, and all the early prophetic oracles of Israel were expressed in poetry.)

In the language of faith, as in the arts, the human imagination plays an important role. This does not imply, however, a flight into an unreal world of fantasy. Even the sciences, in spite of their apparent matter-of-factness, depend for their progress upon man's imagination. Most of the great milestones in scientific advance have been achieved, not by rational calculations and deductions, but by brilliant leaps of the human imagination. The greatest scientists are those who have had the most fertile imaginations, combined with the integrity of scientific method. It may be said that the so-called laws of nature have come to expression through the success man has had to date in directing his imagination to particular fields of inquiry. These laws, like the human language in which they are expressed, are, in part, man's own products, as their verbal expression has resulted from the application of his imagination to the world he seeks to know.

If imagination plays such a vital role even in such sciences as physics and astronomy, where man can so clearly be an objective spectator, how much more must man depend upon his imagination when seeking to understand the questions of human existence, in which he is at the same time an active participant. As the man of faith uses his imagination to develop a language adequate to express the experience of faith, he may use a variety of modes, such as ecstatic utterances, prayers and hymns. But perhaps the word which most adequately describes the nature of the language of faith is myth. In the ancient world it was in myth that the human imagination reached out in an attempt to understand the truth of human existence.

It is a great pity that the word 'myth' has for many people become synonymous with a story which is untrue. This has come about because the new world has so decisively abandoned the mythological elements of the old world. But in Chapter 8 it was suggested that the abandonment of the mythological elements did not necessarily mean the end of 'myth'. We may freely admit that there is a danger that, if we continue to use the word 'myth', it may be mistakenly assumed that we are attempting to restore the mythological view of ancient man. Some Christians quite understandably want to avoid the term 'myth' on the grounds that the Christian heritage is grounded in history and not in mythology. But on the other hand there is one thing which the man of the new world still has in common with ancient man and that is his humanity. Scientific language has replaced myth for the understanding of physical phenomena, but it has not replaced poetry and art as the expression of the human spirit. Myth, properly understood, can serve contemporary man, as well as it served ancient man, for the verbal expression of the response of the human spirit to the environment of his existence.

The element which most clearly distinguishes myth from an historical narrative is the reference at some point to God. When we say that Jesus was crucified at Jerusalem we are making an historical statement. But when we say that the Word of God became flesh and dwelt among us, we are speaking in terms of myth. Indeed if the life of Jesus is to be related to God in any way at all, then we are forced to move out of the language of history and enter the medium of myth. For the historian *per se* can say nothing about God. The historian may evaluate the evidence relating to the empty tomb, but Peter's statement of faith, "This Jesus God raised up", is outside the scope of historical inquiry. Peter has drawn upon the medium of myth to affirm the faith into which he had been led, and he had little choice, if his faith was to find verbal expression.

The use of myth as the language of faith does not turn the myth into history. But neither can it be categorically stated that myth is untrue, unreal and meaningless, as long as it continues to be meaningful to, and to win the response of faith from, those to whom it is spoken. For this reason, however, myth in the new world will be markedly different in some respects from myth in the ancient world. Whereas the ancient myth bore all the marks of the mythological world to which it was orientated, the myth which the man of faith in the new world finds meaningful will be orientated to the human situation as contemporary man understands it, and it could even be called a 'demythologized myth' or 'historically-grounded myth'.

The Bible itself helps to make the difference clear. As we noted earlier, the story of the Garden of Eden almost certainly had a prototype in ancient mythology, where its original theme seems likely to have been man's search for immortality. But Israel turned the story round. It is no longer about the unseen world of the gods, but about men in the world of here and now. As *Adam* is simply the

Hebrew word for 'man', the story is about man and his wife, and becomes one of the most penetrating narratives ever written about human self-understanding.

There is narrated here with vivid clarity the subtle steps by which man in his daily experience is led into temptation and error, for reasons which at the time appear quite convincing. Then in a flash the stark reality of what he has done comes home to him. His plausible reasoning is now shown up and leaves him defenceless. He is left naked before the truth. The guilty couple feel even the need to hide from each other by clothing themselves. But this is but the premonition of the ultimate confrontation with God, for He it is with whom all men have ultimately to reckon.

Yet the story does not tell us who God is, but only what He says. Man hears himself called to give account. He tries to make excuses for himself. The man blames his wife, and the wife blames the serpent, which here represents that mysterious factor in the human situation, which is felt to be essentially different from the true self. Israel then linked up the judgment consequent upon man's guilt with the mysterious pains of childbirth and the frustrations which confront the honest toiler.

This is an imaginative story, about man rather than about the gods, and consequently it differs from the ancient myths. But it is a story which still refers to God, and consequently includes the element of true myth. Not only was this myth meaningful within Israel and the former generations of Christian believers, but also to us living in the new world, three thousand years later, it still speaks powerfully, as it lights up for us our human nature and our human predicament.

But Israel demythologized very few ancient myths in this way. She turned to a different source as the seedbed of the new form of myth, and that was the human historical scene. Let us take the sagas of Abraham and Jacob. We do not know for certain that these two men ever lived. What Old Testament scholarship has managed to show is the probability that Abraham and Jacob were two of the more important chieftains who led migrating tribes from upper Mesopotamia to Canaan, and that some of the stories now gathered in the sagas originated around these historical figures.

But about the original figures we really know practically nothing, for Israel kept reinterpreting the original stories, as well as adding new ones, in order to express in these sagas the hopes and convictions which Israel came to believe about herself as a people. Abraham was adopted as the father of Israel and came to portray the destiny to which Israel felt called. Abraham was seen as the very model of faith and obedience, and captured the imagination of

Israel more and more as time went on, with the result that in the New Testament we find Paul using him as the example of the true believer.

In contrast with this the Jacob saga portrays the real and all too frail and human Israel. Much is made of Jacob's craftiness and deceptive tricks, but he was a man who was being chastened and reformed by God, as the change of name from Jacob to Israel eventually makes clear. The story of how Jacob returns from a far country to face the brother he wronged, and how he wrestles all night with an unknown mysterious assailant, provides a penetrating picture of Israel's own encounter with YHWH all through her history.

In contrast with the ancient myths these sagas are drawn from ancestral traditions. But though they are set in the tangible historical world, they describe men who encounter YHWH at all the strategic points in their lives. It is the reference to God in these narratives which leads them into the realm of myth. These sagas of Abraham and Jacob may be said to be myths which express the faith into which Israel found herself called by reason of her encounter with YHWH through the course of history.

Of course even the modern historian must use his imagination. He does not set out to give a full and cinematographic record of all things said and done in the period under review, for that would be neither possible nor valuable. He must select the words and events which, in his judgment, are crucial. He tries to discern the various trends and personal factors at work. Israel's interpreters were doing this too, as they pioneered the concern with history, and that is the strength of the claim that the Christian heritage, in contrast with mythology, is grounded in history. But unlike the historian, the biblical writers moved into the realm of myth, even if sparingly, for only thus could their understanding of history become the expression of their faith.

The chief 'historically-grounded myth' of the Old Testament is the tradition of the Exodus from Egypt and the Covenant at Sinai. As we have already noted, historical research has so far failed to bring to light the historical events which gave rise to this tradition. But even if the historian were able to confirm that an unusual flow of water at the Sea of Reeds trapped Pharaoh's army and enabled the Israelites to make good their escape, it is beyond the scope of the historian to deny or confirm that it was none other than YHWH who brought Israel out of Egypt. Even if the historian were able to confirm that at a certain mountain, called Sinai, the Israelites celebrated a ceremony which they believed to be a covenant with YHWH, it is beyond his scope to deny or confirm that YHWH was in fact a party to the covenant. So while the Exodus tradition may in a real sense be grounded in history, its essential importance for Israel is actually the mythical element in it. It is this which constitutes Israel's own affirmation of faith.

Let us now turn to the 'historically-grounded myth' of the New Testament, the one that forms the focal point for the whole of the Christian Bible, and in which is expressed the heart of the Christian faith. We have already seen the difficulty of recovering reliable knowledge of the Jesus of history. But even if the historian were able to present to us with some confidence the historical data of the man Jesus, the real heart of the Christian Gospel would still be left untouched by historical inquiry. Not even historical confirmation of the Virgin Birth or the empty tomb, should either be achieved, would offer convincing proof of what the New Testament sets out to affirm. The focal point of attention is not the life and ministry of Jesus, but his death and resurrection. The New Testament claims, that Jesus died on the cross for men's salvation, and that he rose in victory to ascend to the right hand of God, are outside the historian's field of reference. They are affirmations of faith, in which the first-century Christians found it necessary to move into myth for the joyful proclamation of the Gospel. The New Testament story of Jesus becomes the centre of the Christian faith only as it *is* transformed into an 'historically-grounded myth', for myth is the language of faith.

Historical inquiry can show with high probability that Jesus was a good man, who delivered some powerful preaching to his fellow-Jews, and who so roused the opposition of the authorities that they tried to silence him by putting him to death. But this is not what the New Testament is primarily concerned to profess. That is why the picture of Jesus as the great teacher of the fatherhood of God and the brotherhood of man falls far short of the New Testament witness. The only way of expressing the faith of the apostles is to use myth, the language of faith. Because the disciplined study of history has helped us to distinguish between history and myth, and to come to the tentative conclusion that the stories of the Virgin Birth, the Transfiguration, the Resurrection and the Ascension are mythical in character, this does not mean that the faith which they have traditionally expressed and conveyed is thereby undermined.

The way to test the truth and validity of the myth is to ask whether it adequately performs its role as the language of faith. Does the historically-grounded myth of Jesus Christ communicate faith from the believer to the unbeliever? It can hardly be disputed that up until the present time it certainly has done this. But some may wish to argue that it was only because the mythical elements in the

Gospel of Christ were assumed to be historical that it in fact did have the power to communicate faith. It is not quite as simple as that. For one thing it is anachronistic to press back into the past the present distinctions between history and myth which only the new world has helped us to clarify.

But the main answer to this objection is that faith is not the kind of response to which the believer is led by means of rational argument or the production of incontestable historical evidence. Faith is caught from those who already possess it. The evidence for faith is not in the Gospel story, whether it be called myth or not, but in the man of faith himself. The Gospel story is not a self-authenticating demonstration of its own validity. It is the verbal medium by which the man of faith attempts to communicate to the unbeliever his own understanding of faith.

There is a certain parallel between the sagas of Abraham and the Gospel story. Both are grounded in history, and yet in both the imagination of the believer has moulded the original stories to communicate faith and hope. Abraham became the personal symbol of the promise of God concerning the destiny to which Israel was called. The mental picture of the risen and ascended Christ, which the imagination of the Christian believer developed from the memories of the crucified Jesus of history and from the initial apostolic experience, expressed the sense of faith, hope and victory to which the believer had been led.

In each generation each individual Christian moulds his own mental image of the Christ of faith in the light of his contemporary thought and experience. This is mostly done unconsciously, but even when a man becomes aware of what he is doing, it need not stop him, for man must use his imagination to reach self-understanding. But whereas the myth-making of ancient man had no boundaries set for it, the Christian believer is being continually recalled to the biblical witness to the Jesus of History and the apostolic testimony to the Christ of faith. That is the importance of calling the Christian Gospel an historically-grounded myth.

If man is to live, he must find faith. If man is to have faith, it will be caught from those who have faith, and communicated to him in myth, the language of faith. Within the human race the people of Israel pioneered the way of faith which is our heritage, and there is no more powerful myth than the story of the Christ of faith.

CHAPTER 17

God as the Ground of Faith

Whenever we talk about the relationship of God with the scene of human history, we move out of the field of history, as it is commonly understood, and enter the medium of myth. This has led us to justify the use of myth in the new world, partly on the very ground that without it we cannot express our faith in terms of God's concern with the world. But on what grounds are we justified in speaking about God at all?

Throughout most of the Christian era the reality of either gods or God could be taken for granted not only among Christians, but also among the non-Christians to whom the Christian Gospel was proclaimed. Through the Middle Ages and down to quite recent times, theologians believed that, if pressed to do so, they could prove the existence of God on rational grounds. There was usually no need for this however, except as a theological exercise, since the presence of a powerful and authoritative church and the possession of an infallible Bible were usually sufficient to re-awaken faith, if ever believers were faced with doubts.

But today in the new world the most basic premise of the Christian faith has been widely challenged. In proclaiming the Gospel, the Christian can no longer assume that he has a common link with his hearers in some kind of God-belief which forms the basis for the communication of the Christian faith. The Christian is being challenged to show that when he uses religious language, and in particular, when he uses the word 'God', he is speaking in a meaningful way, and is not simply repeating an archaic form of words which belonged to the old world, and which is no more relevant to the new world than goblins and fairies.

It is not simply a matter of debating whether God exists or not, for this begs the basic question of what is meant by the word 'God'. Even the Bible does not hesitate to declare that what some people mean by 'God' is no reality at all. As with all words of the language that man has slowly evolved, the meaning of 'God' is only grasped and appreciated when it is read or heard in the context of human discourse. The word 'God' means what the user of the word wants to make it mean. All of us use words in slightly different ways and impute to them slightly different meanings. Language is not nearly as exact and precise as we often imagine.

But we could not communicate with one another at all by means of language unless for most words there were some commonly accepted meaning, however general. For this reason, we never start a discussion of God with a *tabula rasa*. We ourselves are the products of a culture which has itself been largely shaped by the Christian faith. The language we have inherited from our fathers has already given some kind of content to our use of the word 'God', whether we regard ourselves as believers or non-believers. But within the limits set by the cultural background of the world, there are still considerable differences in the connotation the word has for each of us. If we are believers, we have emphasized those aspects which enable us to adopt a positive and accepting attitude to the word. If we are non-believers, we have fastened our attention upon those aspects which cause us to adopt a negative and rejecting attitude.

Our first task is to examine the way in which the Bible bears verbal witness to God. Here it is to be noted that the Bible does not confine itself to one word. As we have seen, there is the untranslatable proper name YHWH, which was Israel's most treasured word to point to the reality, who, they believed, had delivered them from Egyptian bondage. But they did not hesitate to use other words, such as the untranslatable *El Shaddai*, and those translated as ,'God', 'Lord', the 'God of Abraham, Isaac and Jacob', the 'Holy One of Israel'. The Old Testament goes to some trouble to make it clear that all these words refer to the one reality. Another important aspect of the biblical talk of God is that He is not simply 'God', but so often 'our God', the 'God of our fathers', the 'God and Father of the Lord Jesus Christ'.

Next we must note that there is considerable diversity in the ways in which the Bible describes how God manifests Himself to man. We have already noted the growing reluctance to speak of God in anthropomorphic terms. Theophanies gave way to angel talk, and angel talk to visions, and visions to the hearing of the Word of God in the inner ear. The Bible reflects no embarrassment about this variety of usage. In the New Testament we find the apostolic church talking about God in some quite new ways. Yet even though the differences in usage between Old Testament and New Testament caused some second century Christians to conclude that two different realities were referred to, the apostolic church was adamant, that it was none other than the God of Israel who had spoken to men in Jesus.

Now this variety of usage in the biblical talk of God (and modern scholarship has shown that the biblical statements cannot all be neatly fitted together into a systematic whole, in the way some earlier Christian thinkers assumed that to be possible) makes it clear that the Bible is not wedded to any particular form of words concerning God. The words themselves do not contain the reality to which they refer; they are pointers. The biblical words are used to point to the deepest reality in the experience of man.

What is the relevance to us of the God-pointing language of the Bible? This is the same as asking, "What is the deepest reality for our experience as men of the new world, and is it the same reality as that to which the Bible points?" We have seen that when the Bible is read against the background of the ancient mythological cultures, it is found to be pointing in a different direction. Whereas they pointed to the pantheon of gods in their unseen heavenly world, the Bible pointed to one who was in no way to be identified with the gods of ancient man, but who was known to them in the sphere of human history as the deepest reality confronting them there. This concern with the human scene finally led attention to be focussed on Jesus of Nazareth, a man of history, who lived and died as other men do, and yet one in whom the God of Israel confronted men in a unique way.

Even though the Bible was pointing away from the gods of ancient man, it was still forced to use the God-language of ancient man. For this reason conservative Christians maintain that if we dispense with the concept of God as a supernatural being dwelling in heaven, we are rejecting the biblical witness. But the biblical witness must be read in its own context, and when this is done, we must look for the direction in which the faith of Israel was moving, not for the mythological remnants still present in its expression.

Now just as Israel carried through the theological spring-cleaning proper to her time, so we, if we are to be faithful to her lead, must pursue the reformation of God-talk appropriate to our time. One aspect of God-talk, for example, which is overdue for elimination is that which tries to look for evidence of God in the areas of human ignorance, and which seeks to use him as the explanation of all we do not understand. There is no room for the 'God of the gaps' in the new world, nor is this the God of whom the Bible speaks. The God of Israel met men not on the borders of life, but at the centre, at the point of deepest significance.

Another aspect of God-talk that must go is that which looks to God as a source of super-human power, who can be persuaded, and even cajoled, by the appeal of prayer, to perform those desires of man, which man cannot manage for himself. There is not all that much difference between the dancing of the prophets of Baal before their altar in the hope that their god would vindicate them, and the all-night prayer relay which seeks a glorious harvest of souls at the mass meeting of the visiting evangelist.

But when we have allowed for the various images of God which ought certainly to vanish, because they are the remnants of ancient mythology, we are still left with the question of God-talk itself. Must even the very word 'God' be now abandoned? This is a vital current issue. It may be that, more and more in the new world, men may find they can speak of the deepest reality of their experience without any need to use the God-talk inherited from our fathers. If so, we must listen appreciatively, remembering that, because all human language is relative and limited, we must not let any one word or group of words assume the qualities of an absolute, for that would be a return to the idolatry from which the faith of our fathers sought to deliver us. The Bible shows no concern when its writers were led to replace an earlier name or form of words by a new expression, and consequently it cannot be said that either the Bible or Christian tradition has made one particular doctrine of God or one form of words sacrosanct.

Some of the most fruitful thoughts about the role of God-belief in the new world have come from Dietrich Bonhoeffer (1906–45), a German theologian who was executed in a German prison a few days before VE Day, for having taken part in a plot against Hitler's life. His most creative contributions are found, though only in seed-form, in his *Letters and Papers from Prison.* He spoke of our era as 'man's coming of age', and said, "God is teaching us that we must live as men who can get along very well without him". While we cannot say how Bonhoeffer himself would have developed the implications of these phrases, let us attempt to apply them to the question of God in the new world.

In the life of each man there is a long period of preparation and growth before maturity is reached, before he comes of age. In his pre-natal existence the embryonic person passes through various stages remarkably similar to those by which the whole race has developed by biological evolution. In infancy, childhood and adolescence, he passes through stages which find some striking parallels in the sociological evolution of mankind. A person owes his very existence to his parents, and inherits from them such traits as can be transmitted biologically. At birth he is still wholly dependent upon them. In the course of time he receives from them the language and the heritage of culture which enable him to develop his human potential. All that a person owes to his parents and to the cultural environment of his birth cannot be overemphasized, and yet it belongs to his very personhood that he becomes steadily independent.

Then he comes of age. The wise parent has been leading his child to the point where he can fend for himself. In coming of age the adolescent recognizes that he must stand on his own feet, and not be looking to his parents to extricate him from the problems and difficulties into which his ineptness and weakness lead him. Parenthood, insofar as it means the exercise of power and control, aims at making itself unnecessary. Yet at the very point where the young adult realizes that now he is free and no longer within the reins of parental control, he begins to find, though often slowly, that much of his parents is with him still. But now it is within him, prompting, guiding and stimulating him from within his own real self.

Now let us turn to the fatherhood of God. The Bible affirms with clarity that we are dependent for our very existence on the fatherhood of God. The traits of our humanity we have inherited from him, for we are made in his likeness. We may see the infancy of the human race, as the long period of man's origins when he was completely at the mercy of his environment. In the mythological culture he recognized his helplessness and looked to the mysterious unseen forces for the things he could not achieve for himself.

The whole Judeo-Christian heritage, from whose roots the new world has sprung, may be regarded as the medium by which God the Father has been leading the human race to its coming of age. The New Testament proclaimed Jesus Christ to be the new man, in whom the nature of God was so fully to be seen that he could be called the 'Son of God', The very significance men saw in Jesus was that by his coming, men should be enabled to come into their own. "To all who received him, who believed in his name, he gave power to become children of God." The letter to the Ephesians claims that the gift of Christ enables men to attain 'to mature manhood, to the measure of the stature of the fulness of Christ'.

If it is of the very nature of the fatherhood of God that he should be leading his children to mature sonship, then we can see some point in saying that we must learn to live without God in the world. This is the maturity of sonship to which God the Father is calling us, and for which he has prepared us by means of the very heritage which has led to the advent of the new world. Yet just at the point where we find ourselves assuming full responsibility, free from the restraints of mythological powers, we become slowly aware that it is He, the God of our fathers, who is in fact prompting, guiding and influencing us from within. The man of faith lives in the new world without appealing to the ancient gods of heaven, for the very spirit of God is within him.

There is a final point from the analogy. The truly mature son does not abandon his father when he learns to stand on his own feet, but on the contrary, with his increasing maturity, he becomes more aware of all that he owes to his parentage, and is increasingly grateful. The test of whether man in the new world has come of age is seen first of all in his ability to shoulder full responsibility for his life, and secondly in the recognition of all that he owes to the fatherhood of God to whom is due praise and thanksgiving.

Some may have concluded, on hearing the phrases quoted from Bonhoeffer, that 'living without God in the world' quickly leads to the cessation of all God-talk. With Bonhoeffer himself it certainly was not so. On the contrary, his letters are full of it, and reflect the life of a man of deep faith, and full of gratitude to God. This may help us to see why the Bible, in spite of the fact that it was turning men away from the gods of mankind's infancy, was quite vigorous in retaining God-talk to point to the deepest reality man encounters in his historical existence.

What men of faith may choose to do, even in the quite near future, concerning this dilemma of the language of faith, is yet not clear. The continued use of the word 'God' with all its associations and images from the old world always constitutes a temptation to turn back in the direction of mythology, and that leads to idolatry, which has always been the church's greatest weakness. One can readily appreciate why some have been searching for new ways of expressing the attitude of faith towards the deepest reality man encounters, that reality to which the Bible points by means of God-language.

But in abandoning the biblical language of faith there lies another danger. It so easily leads to a humanism in which man becomes his own measure and consequently his own god. This is idolatry turned inside out. The more man sees himself as a self-made man, with no one to thank for it but himself, the more he turns into a demon, and of this the history of man has already seen many examples. The great deficiency in absolute humanism in the long run is that it is dehumanizing. The deepest reality we encounter in human existence is not our own image in the mirror, for that is no encounter at all. For this reason no better language has yet appeared in the new world to replace that which we have received from the heritage that has made us.

As we listen to the witness of the Bible, we may be inclined to think, at first, that this is no more than the voice of the human Israel which points us away from the gods of idolatry as the first step in man's self-emancipation. But Israel shouts to us that this is none of their doing. The prophets affirm in no uncertain terms that Israel is a nation of stumblers and idolators, but it is the Word of YHWH out of the burning bush, out of the mountain, out of the unknown, to which they bear witness.

The 'this-worldliness' and 'down-to-earthness' which made Israel's faith so distinctive, came to a consummation in the man Jesus. In wildly ecstatic ways, and with all the impreciseness and lack of logical consistency which goes with that kind of unbelievably good news, the New Testament wants to say to us that here is man's chance to become free and to achieve his full human potential. Yet even while it ventures to talk about this man in terms of the God-language of faith, the New Testament does not hesitate to describe this Jesus as a real man and one who points to Him who sent him.

To the extent that the new world may be described as man's coming of age, we must be ready for all the refinements it necessitates for the way we talk about God. But if we dispense with God-talk altogether, we may find that we have not achieved the freedom of maturity at all, but rather lost it by confining our discourse to such limits as no longer allow room for the human spirit to breathe and move. Words like 'God', 'divinity', 'holiness' arose admittedly in the mythological context. But the human spirit needs these words, for true it is that in God 'we live and move and have our being'.

It may well be objected that we still have not made clear what is meant by the word 'God'. That is true. By God-talk we are pointing to the deepest reality we encounter, to that which concerns us ultimately. But we do not know what that is. The God that is known is an idol. The God who can be defined, is no God. It is of the essence of human existence that man lives not by knowledge, but by faith. It is by faith that man is led to fulfilment and ultimate destiny, and God is the ground of his faith.

CHAPTER 18

Hope as the Goal of Faith

In addition to faith, hope is another basic ingredient essential for human existence, for man cannot live indefinitely without some form of hope. But faith and hope are quite closely linked, for, as the New Testament says, it is faith which gives substance to our hopes. Faith is born out of the heritage of past experience, and is created and fostered in us by the Word of God which is communicated to us through those who already possess faith. But insofar as faith, as the attitude of present trust, is necessarily involved also with the future, it gives rise to hope. Hope may be called the goal of faith, for it is that unseen destination in the future which gives direction to the present life of obedience of the man of faith.

Just as in the case of faith, the Christian can claim no monopoly of hope as a human experience. Hope begins to grow in us from early childhood, and is necessarily related to the confined and immature context of the child's life. Hope assumes definite shape in the form of Christmas presents and birthday parties, prowess in a sport, and occasionally, even high academic attainment. The child becomes increasingly aware that he too will grow up to be a man, and, in the ever increasing horizon of his life, hope takes on maturer forms. In late adolescence, hope concerns itself frequently with the choice of a life career. Not all people experience hope with the same degree of clarity or intensity. Some may not think much about the future at all, but may be content to drift from day to day, and eventually from job to job. There is probably some incipient form of hope in all, but where it lacks intensity, life seems to be the poorer, for such a person is not reaching out to his full potential.

It is when we look at the meaning of life within its broadest possible context that we become concerned with hope at its deepest level. The simple and mundane objects which stimulate men to hope in their earlier years are concrete manifestations, within limited horizons, of that basic attitude which gives zest, interest and purpose to life. Just as the word 'faith' describes an attitude in man himself, as well as that which fosters the attitude, so 'hope' has been used to refer both to a human attitude, and to that which prompts the attitude, namely that to which his mind and spirit look forward.

The community of believers in whom the Judeo-Christian faith has manifested itself in successive generations, has been most full of vigour and vitality when it has been looking forward in hope. But though the basic attitude of hope may remain fundamentally the same, the form in which it is understood and verbally expressed may vary considerably from one generation to another. The hope which spurred on the Hebrew slaves from Egypt towards a land flowing with milk and honey could not also be the hope of the later Israelites who had entered into possession of Canaan, for hope always lies in the future. It concerns that which is unseen and unknown, that which is not yet. The hope of the community of faith has sometimes taken shape in worldly terms and sometimes it has been of an other-worldly form. It is a commentary on the other-worldly character of the orthodox form of Christianity we have inherited, that the very term 'Christian hope' has come to be used almost exclusively for what the Christian expects to enter into on the other side of death.

Modern study of the Bible has brought the discovery that the Christian hope is not at all exclusively tied to an other-worldly form; indeed, as we have seen, that is just what it had started to lead men away from. To see how the man of faith, living in the new world, is to express his hope, we can do no better than start with the biblical expressions of hope. The first such expression is quite near the beginning. By means of the story of the great flood, in which things were described as being so bad that the human race was all but annihilated, Israel was taught to see in the rainbow a sign that God would never again send such a catastrophe to blot out mankind. This is Israel's way of saying that there are signs of hope set in the life of the tangible world itself, and they are there for all men to read, if they have eyes to see. Something similar is expressed in our proverbial saying, "Hope springs eternal in the human breast." This is not the whole of the Christian hope, but it must not be scornfully dismissed as beneath the Christian's notice. This hope belongs to man's very nature. Man is a creature who has some hope already built into him, so that he often keeps on hoping in spite of himself, and for reasons he knows not why. It is this hope which is already set in man by his Creator, that is nurtured and cultivated by the Judeo-Christian heritage.

So while the Bible starts at this point, it goes on to show that hope takes on a new and unexpected quality as man finds himself addressed by the Word of God and called to the life of faith. We have already noted that running through the patriarchal sagas there is the thread of hope, expressed in the form of the double promise of land and progeny. What is easily overlooked is that the original promise to Abraham made no appeal to his personal self-interest. Abraham did not live to see either of his hopes come to fruition, and he was at no point led to expect that he would. Yet it was a hope that could claim his attention and interest to the point where he took the steps of faith and obedience so necessary for the fulfilment. In this story of Abraham, Israel expressed some of her understanding of the nature of hope.

Moses is another whose hope undoubtedly came to fruition, and yet not in any way which centred upon his own personal well-being. He was a man who spent his life in leading Israel to the land of promise. But he himself did not enter. As tradition has it, God led him to the top of Mount Nebo and showed him all the land from Dan in the north to Judah in the south, and then said, "I have let you see it with your eyes, but you shall not go over there". Moses died and God buried him. Yet in the New Testament story of the Transfiguration of Jesus, it was the Moses who had died who was said to have appeared, along with the Elijah who had never died. Thus the biblical language of myth sets out the victory in altruistic hope.

It is not surprising that the intensity of hope waxes and wanes from one generation to another. For wandering homeless nomads, and for oppressed slaves in Egypt, hope was experienced with an intense urgency. But when life is marked by comfort, ease and present satisfaction, hope may be relegated to the periphery of man's concerns. Through much of the period from David to the fall of Jerusalem, Israel's life was not marked by the concern with hope, any more than is the life of the affluent society of the west today.

The Babylonian exile was destined to bring forth the re-birth of hope, In the early days Ezekiel reports that the exiles were saying, "Our bones are dried up, and our hope is lost; we are clean cut off." But a generation later the unknown prophet was bringing comforting news which did much to rekindle their hope. In spite of varied fortunes and successive forms of imperialistic domination, that hope remained alive. It was experienced most vividly when the outlook was darkest. The two books of the Bible, which are the most vivid and triumphant expressions of hope, came out of periods of fierce persecution. They are Daniel and Revelation.

There is no need to sketch again what has already been said about the hope which formed the setting for the advent of Jesus, namely, the new age to be ushered in by God's anointed king. The Death and Resurrection of Jesus became the focal point for the full consummation of that new age which they hoped very shortly to witness. But a hope involving an imminent event cannot retain its convincing power over a period which begins to stretch out indefinitely. It was inevitable that it should find another mode of expression, and this it did, as we have already seen.

Again in our day, the form of expression of the Christian hope is undergoing quite radical change, for, as we have seen, the orthodox picture of it we have inherited from the Middle Ages has been gradually losing its forcefulness with the advent of the new world. In addition to its mythological framework, there is a second and perhaps even more serious defect in it that is now beginning to make itself more evident. The promise of a life of eternal bliss in heaven above, and the threat of the torment of eternal punishment in the hell below, proclaimed as the two alternatives which faced man as his eternal destiny, frequently had the unfortunate effect of leading men in the direction of self-centredness.

Man was quite rightly given little encouragement to think that his eternal salvation could be won by his own unaided efforts, for it was the gift of divine grace. But when the hearer of the Gospel came to the point of decision, that is, to accept or reject it, it was taken for granted that this should be made on the basis of spiritual self-interest. The form of the Christian hope encouraged a man to be concerned primarily about his own soul. It was put to him (and still often is) that to embrace the faith and give allegiance to Christ as Lord and Saviour was in the long run in his own interests.

It cannot be denied that this form of hope often led men to great acts of self-denial; yet the very motives being fostered to promote it had in them a strong element of self-gain. If a man becomes a philanthropist with the deliberate intention of expecting to see his name in the New Year honours, we rightly feel that there is something hollow about his ostensible concern for others. If a man denies himself comforts and pleasures in this life in order to be assured of happiness in the eternal hereafter, he still does not avoid being self-centred. His self-centredness has merely taken a subtle, spiritual form.

The first thing that needs to be said about the shape of Christian hope within the new world, is that it must recover and embody that selfless concern that marked the hope of ancient Israel. In the story of Abraham, Israel recognized that the fulfilment of hope lies far beyond the limits of any one man's mortal life. Because Abraham represented the man who saw this, but who nevertheless obeyed, he was a man who embodied both faith and hope, and later generations gave him the unique title of 'friend of God'.

In the new secular world, the only recovery of hope possible is that which is prepared to surrender all concern for the self, whether material or spiritual, out of love and concern for the common good. The hope that led Moses on was not for himself, but for his people. His hope was not shattered because he only got as far as seeing the promised land from afar, before he died and was buried in an unknown grave. His hope came to a glorious fulfilment, so that Israel, centuries later, recognized this man of vision by saying, "There has not arisen a prophet since in Israel like Moses, whom YHWH knew face to face."

The later prophets were stirred by a vision of hope, in which they looked to YHWH to renew the world by the abolition of war, famine and plague, by reconciling not only bitter and hostile men, but even the very animals that lived by preying upon one another, and it did not even occur to those prophets to ask what would be their own personal place in that new world to which they looked in hope. Hosea suffered a domestic disaster. Jeremiah was persecuted by his own family, and trod an increasingly lonely path which ended in death in Egypt. Yet their hope in God did not vanish. Jeremiah's own experience set the pattern for those psalmists whose words have kindled hope in the hearts of many generations since. The New Testament says of the prophets that even though 'they did not receive what was promised' they remained steadfast in faith and hope.

The most thorough-going expression of hope in a fully secular form is to be found today in Marxist Communism, and no Christian can afford to ignore it. It is being recognized a little more readily today by at least some Marxists and some Christians, that the Communist concern for the welfare of the whole human society, including in particular that of the worker, and the Communist hope for a renewed world with a classless society, find their roots in the Judeo-Christian heritage, and especially the new-world-hope of the prophets of Israel. Most of the deviations from the orthodox Christian stream have arisen because orthodoxy has neglected some essential. The rapid rise and spread of Communism must be accepted by Christians as the most seriously challenging deviant form of the Judeo-Christian heritage, just as, in the eighth century, the rise of Islam came about because of the tendency for Christian trinitarian doctrine to revert to polytheism, adding weight to Muhammed's call for a pure monotheism.

The hostility that broke out and still exists between Christian and Marxist is equally understandable from both sides. The Marxist felt little mercy for an ecclesiastical organization which had itself become an instrument of power, aiding and abetting those who had much, and showing scant concern for the present welfare of those who had little. The Christian became horrified by the political aspirations and methods of those who were fired with concern for the masses, but who had little concern for the individual. Yet, in this struggle, the faith and hope of some Marxists have put to shame the devotion of many a Christian.

Today's Christian finds it a bitter pill to swallow to be told that he must learn a lesson from the Communist and his secular hope for society, but long ago a prophet of Israel ventured to speak of the arch-enemy, Assyria, as an instrument in the hand of God, and another dared to name a foreign emperor as the very Messiah sent by YHWH. Communism has challenged Christians to rediscover that element of their heritage which concerns itself with the renewal of human society in the here and now. Until this is done, there can be no reshaping and revitalizing of the Christian hope for men of the new world. Christians must rediscover the this-worldly hope which has always been there in their best-known prayer, "Thy kingdom come. Thy will be done in earth as it is in heaven". The renewal of the world is the Christian hope, and even though, because of our mortal limited lives, like Moses we do not live to witness the consummation, but see it only in embryo, it is sufficient reward to have been used by God in this mighty process of the redemption of the world from the evil, suffering and misery to which man himself has contributed.

Only after we have recognized the Christian hope in this form, are we in a position to ask the humanist or the Marxist if his work for the renewal of society and for the future generations of mankind actually exhausts the meaning of hope for the man of the new world. What are we to say of the human spirit? And is not life more than food, and the body more than clothing? If so, what are we to make of death? Is the embalming of the dead body of the pioneering hero of the new society the only answer that secular man can give to the quest of the human spirit?

Admittedly there is no returning to the picture of immortal life in a supernatural heaven. The man of the new world finds the prospect of an interminable life of heavenly bliss as horrifying to contemplate, as medieval man found the prospect of eternal torment in hell. If man seeks any continuation of life, it is a continuation of the life he knows here, accompanied by all the interests and vexations of movement and change. But he knows also that this life comes to an end.

At this point knowledge takes us no further in our pursuit of the meaning of life and death. The humanist stops, for he can go no further. The Christian proceeds, but he can do so only by faith, and he can speak about the eternal nature of hope only in the language of faith. In the life of faith the Christian has come to find in the human spirit qualities which have a deathlessness about them. He finds himself addressed by the Word of Him who is eternal, and he is led to an attitude of hope which is eternal. It is not primarily hope for himself, but hope for the human spirit, hope for the world, hope for all men, past, present and future. This hope has clothed itself in the past in the picture of the new age, and then in the picture of the blissful heaven. The truth existing in these pictures is not their now outworn form but the spirit of hope they have been used to express.

The man of faith finds himself to be a man of hope, for no adequate or demonstrable reasons at all. In the language of the world, Jesus is dead. But in the language of faith, Jesus is risen. And because He is risen, the world is a different place. Moses and the prophets are dead. But it is not the end. The saints and martyrs are dead. But it is not the end. We shall die – really die. But it is not the end. All men and the whole world have only one end, and that end, so faith enables us to say, is in God, who has neither beginning nor end.

CHAPTER 19

Love as the Life of Faith

One of the most inspired chapters in all of Paul's letters is that in which, as if in a sudden mood of wild abandon, he sets aside all his theological argument and goes straight to the heart of the Christian life in what has been called a magnificent hymn of love. It is at the end of this that he links together the three basic realities of human experience, in which man senses that which is eternal. There are three things, he says, which abide, or last for ever. They are faith, hope and love, but the greatest of the three is love.

We have already seen that faith and hope are closely related. But even these, so far as their Christian expression is concerned, lose their intrinsic value unless they are directed by, and expressed in love. As in the case of both faith and hope, we must recognize that the Christian heritage has no monopoly of the practice of love, for it, too, is basic to the human condition. It is out of the love of a man and a woman that the human being receives his very existence. (The fact that sexual attraction may, in some cases, contain no element of love in it at all, but be only an act of lust, must not be allowed to blind us to the love that can be, and indeed ought to be, in the marriage relationship.) This is important because it makes it clear that the family, or basic human community, in which the newly born infant learns to take the first steps in faith and hope, is itself created by love and should continue to be a community visibly demonstrating love. The family setting shows us the human situation in miniature. From this setting each person receives his humanity, including the ingredients essential for human existence, namely, faith, hope and love.

Wherever humanity reaches some maturity of expression, a high value comes to be placed on love. And wherever love is to be found, and at whatever level it is expressed, it is to be recognized for what it is and valued. It is false, and indeed presumptuous, to suggest, as too frequently it has been done, that only Christians know anything about love. Jesus himself is reported to have acknowledged that even the despised tax-collectors of his day loved those who were close to them and who loved them in return. It is a matter for rejoicing that love is so basic to our humanity, that it has often come to light in unexpected places and caused faith and hope to be born again.

No one who knows anything at all about Christianity will want to deny that love holds the central place in it. It is the subject of the only two commandments recorded as coming from the lips of Jesus, and finally the New Testament makes the rather astounding affirmation that "God is love". But it is wrong to suppose that Christianity has created love where there was none at all before. What the Christian heritage has done is to focus attention upon it, and then declare that something happened in the advent of Christ which allows love to reach its highest level and full potential.

To see how the Judeo-Christian heritage has come to centre man's attention upon love, we must go a long way back. One of the earliest descriptions of it in Israelite tradition has now become quite proverbial. The quality of the relationship that developed between David and Jonathan was unusual, because, in their situation, ordinary family loyalty, coupled with Saul's intense jealousy of David, should have spelled the end to their friendship. Instead, however, the love of these two for one another attained an eternal quality, and was cemented in a covenant. "And Jonathan made David swear again by his love for him; for he loved him as he loved his own soul."

When Jonathan was later tragically killed in battle, the love of David in mourning is expressed in one of the finest war laments ever written, "I am distressed for you my brother Jonathan; very pleasant have you been to me; your love to me was wonderful, passing the love of women". Even in those early days of Israelite tradition, the level to which human love could ascend was being recognized, and already it was being linked with the love of God. This has not always come out as clearly as it should have done in English translations of the Old Testament, since there is no real equivalent in English for the key word used for it in the Hebrew. It is the word found in the mouth of Jonathan, and rendered in the R.S.V. as "Show me the *loyal love* of YHWH that I may not die."

The prophet Hosea stands out as a milestone in the growing concern for love found in Israelite tradition. Although we cannot be quite certain about the nature of Hosea's relationship with his Wife Gomer, it was probably out of the pain of his own broken marriage, that he came to see that the love of a faithful partner could redeem a situation shattered by infidelity. From the quality of this kind of love in the human situation, Hosea came to discern the nature of the love of YHWH for his people, Israel. As well as using the analogy from marriage, Hosea applied to God the metaphor of fatherly concern, in a way which prefigured the father's love in the parable of the prodigal son. "When Israel was a child, I loved him, and out of Egypt I called my son . . . it was I who taught Ephraim to walk, I took them up in my arms . . . I led them with cords of compassion, with the bands of love . . ."

A century later the Deuteronomic scholars, living under the impact of prophets like Hosea, set love at the centre of all that should mark the life of obedience to which YHWH called Israel. The words of the Jewish Shema, quoted earlier, are immediately followed by the great commandment, "You shall love YHWH your God with all your heart, and with all your soul, and with all your might."

These are but a few of the stepping-stones to be found in the developing tradition of Israel which was destined to lead to the vibrant concern with love manifested in the New Testament. In both the teaching and the person of Jesus, love came out clearly into the centre and at the same time rose to an unprecedented level. Out of the Old Testament Jesus took the two basic commandments about love: the one just quoted from Deuteronomy, and the other which lies hidden in Leviticus among a multitude of lesser injunctions both moral and ceremonial, "You shall love your neighbour as yourself". Jesus showed that these two commandments belong together. The love of God and the love of one's fellowmen, which already possessed an incipient association in the Old Testament, were now explicitly linked together as one. One cannot love God unless one also loves one's fellowmen, and one cannot love one's fellowmen without loving God. A later New Testament writer put it quite strongly; "If anyone says, 'I love God', and hates his brother, he is a liar; for he who does not love his brother whom he has seen, cannot love God whom he has not seen."

But Jesus further showed that love does not consist simply in loving those who respond in love, or in fulfilling certain clearly defined duties of a loving character. Love can be of such a quality that it knows no limits at all. Love reaches out beyond duty, and of its own freewill goes the second mile. It continues even when there is no response. It is prepared to forgive not just seven times, but seventy times seven. It transcends all human barriers and reaches out even to one's fiercest enemies. The love of one's enemies, perhaps more than anything else, vividly demonstrates the unique quality of love to which the Christian heritage points.

Paul's hymn of love brings out this quality in the words which Moffatt rendered as: "Love is very patient, very kind. Love knows no jealousy; love makes no parade, gives itself no airs, is never rude, never selfish, never irritated, never resentful; love is never glad when others go wrong, love is gladdened by goodness, always slow to expose, always eager to believe the best, always hopeful, always patient. Love never disappears."

The parables of the prodigal son and the good Samaritan have long been treasured as the clearest examples used by Jesus to teach the love of God in the one, and the way in which a man should love his neighbour in the other. But Jesus did much more than bring new insights into the nature of love by means of teaching. He lived the love of which he spoke in such a way that the story of his ministry, passion and death has become the classic expression of what love means. That which first became manifest in the human situation, and which was reaching out to higher levels in the lives of David and Jonathan and of Hosea, came to breathtaking expression in Jesus.

So powerful was the impact made by the advent of Jesus that men came quickly to believe that in Jesus the love of God for man, and the love of man for God and his fellows, had become fused together in one and the same human life. The tendency there has been in Christian thought, from quite near the beginning, to depreciate the true humanity of Jesus and to turn him into a divine being, appearing temporarily in the form of man, fails to do justice to the magnificence, indeed the perfection, of that portrayal of love in the human scene. The New Testament holds together in a fine balance the love of God and the love of man. The same Gospel which says, "God so loved the world that he gave his only Son", also puts into the mouth of Jesus, "Greater love has no man than this, that a man lay down his life for his friends." The Johannine writings of the New Testament bring love clearly to the forefront as the theme of the Gospel. The first letter of John speaks of love more than anything else, including this finely worded exhortation:

> Beloved, let us love one another; for love is of God, and he who loves is born of God and knows God. He who does not love does not know God; for God is love. In this the love of God was made manifest among us, that God sent his only Son into the world, so that we might live through him. In this is love, not that we loved God but that he loved us and sent his Son to be the expiation for our sins. Beloved, if God so loved us, we also ought to love one another. No man has ever seen God; if we love one another, God abides in us and his love is perfected in us.

Now while we have maintained that the love which is central to the Christian heritage must not be regarded as wholly different in kind from the love which is basic to the human situation, it must at the same time be said that the advent of Jesus Christ not only demonstrated the highest level to which the activity of love can rise, but actually introduced into the human scene an impetus in the direction of love which was not there before. It is the testimony of the New Testament and of the Christian community through the ages that the Christian Gospel delivers the man of faith from the inertia which so often prevents him from loving his fellows. Christians have always been ready to affirm that this in fact happens, more confidently than they have been able to give reasons to explain it.

Part of the reason is that the Christian faith takes seriously what has been traditionally called the fallen nature of man, namely, that man is a sinful creature, who does not find in himself the power to bring to fulfilment the ideals which attract him. When he repeatedly fails, he is often inclined to give up the struggle. It must be admitted that a certain amount of traditional Christian talk about man's sinfulness has led to an unhealthy and morbid obsession with man's weakness. But even when we allow for this, there still remains to be made an essential self-assessment of our human frailty, and we ignore or evade this at our peril. Whether we like it or not, we must in honesty confess that we fall short of what we see we ought to be; and if we are not too ready to confess this about ourselves, we are usually quick to see it in other people. There is no need to elaborate here the various features of the human scene, such as war, race-riots, family friction, crime, drugs and all the rest, which make it eminently clear that the world of men as a whole stands in need of renewal.

Because of this something in the heart of man, traditionally known as sin, it is unrealistic simply to exhort men to love one another, saying, "If only all men loved one another then all our problems would be solved". Any humanist remedy which relies upon calling man to reform himself, and to live up to the ideal of love, may not be *wholly* without success, but it still leaves man struggling in the chains of his own inadequacy and sheer wilful cussedness. To set before him ideals which he cannot reach, virtually reduces his attempt to a failure before it has begun. The Johannine exhortation quoted above does not do this. It specifically points to something which happened. In the language of faith this is simply that "God sent his only Son in the world, so that we might live through him".

If children ever learn to love their parents, their love is not self-initiated. They love because their parents (or someone *in loco parentis*) first loved them, and, as it were, drew love out of them. What parents do in the family setting, God has done for the human race in the Christ-event which consummated the growing heritage of Israel. So the New Testament says, "We love, because he first loved us". Just how and why the advent of Christ is to be understood as the manifestation of the love of God, and just how it succeeds in drawing the response of love out of men, are questions which will continue to engage the minds of men until the end of time. The fact remains that it did, and still continues to do it. And nothing on earth, in the present or in the future, has the power to obliterate this thing that happened, for the Christ-event is embedded in history.

The whole complex of events to which the Bible bears witness is not something of man's own engineering, but something in which man finds himself encountered by that deepest reality whom he calls God. In this encounter man finds himself, not condemned as he might have expected, but accepted, just as he is, sins and all. The love of God does not say to us, "Reform yourself and all will be forgiven." It simply says, "Son, your sins *are* forgiven." The advent of Christ, an historical event which is none of our doing, says to us that, even before we are reformed, even before we have faith, even before we show penitence, we are accepted. This is something of what it means to say that love is the deepest reality we encounter, and that this love that is God has searched us out.

But now we must face one last question. Some may want to say that the only test of the truth of the Christian proclamation that the advent of Jesus Christ is the manifestation of the love of God, is to be seen in the kind of response which it brings forth from men. Do those, who take to themselves the name of Christian, actually and always demonstrate in their own lives the response of love about which we have been speaking? Here Christians would like to answer with a resounding "Yes!" But most of us know that an unqualified answer would be a piece of hypocrisy. In the long story of the church there is much which seems to belie the claim that love is central to the Christian faith. The New Testament quite frankly recognizes this, but seems also quite clearly to imply, that wherever in the Christian scene we do not see love to be central, clear and unambiguous, then we are not really looking at Christianity. All the rest that goes by the name of Christianity is pseudo-Christianity, hiding the real Gospel from men, and the sooner it fades out of the human picture the better.

Yet perhaps out of Christian love itself, we must learn to refrain from setting ourselves up as judges, particularly on past generations, and look amid the tremendous conglomeration of things that have been said and done in the name of Christianity, for those places and those men and women, where the response of love has come forth and shone in an amazing way. That there have been and still are such, there is absolutely no doubt.

If the present challenge that the new world is bringing to the Christian movement is going to give it the greatest shaking it has had in its two thousand years of history, perhaps we can rejoice. There is much in popular Christianity today that needs to be shaken off, in the form of superstition, hypocrisy, pseudo-piety and spiritual self-centredness. No Christian need fear for the ark of the Lord. In the day of reckoning only those things will remain, which have in them the power to remain because they come of God, and those things are faith, hope and love, and the greatest of the three is love.

CHAPTER 20

The Church as the Community of Faith

The Christian faith comes to visibility in the world, not primarily in creeds, doctrine, liturgical forms or ecclesiastical organization, but in the lives of those people who are experiencing the faith, hope and love, which have the Christian quality. Now one could imagine a person who had a particular kind of faith, which he preferred to keep to himself, or a particular hope which he saw no point in sharing with others, but when it comes to love, we see that by the very nature of this experience, more than one person is involved. The Christian faith, by virtue of the very life of love to which it leads, is essentially a community affair.

We have already referred to the family setting as the basic human community where each new individual is nurtured in faith, hope and love. Just as the family setting brings to every man the basic ingredients of human existence, so the church brings to the believer the distinctively Christian quality of faith, hope and love. The church is the community of Christian faith. All Christian believers have been nurtured by it, and it has sometimes been given the name of mother. Because every Christian in the past and in the present has been brought to faith in one way or another by this community of faith, it follows that the church is not something created or constructed by Christians themselves. The very existence of this community is a witness to the God, who, in fact, did call it into being.

According to the Bible, the Judeo-Christian faith has always been a community affair. At the Exodus from Egypt it was not an individual, nor a group of individuals, but a community, a people, which was delivered from slavery and led to the promised land. The Old Testament is not primarily concerned with the relationships between YHWH and individual Israelites, but with that between YHWH and Israel. The very work *ekklesia* which the New Testament uses for 'church' comes from the Greek Old Testament where it is used to describe the whole 'assembly' of Israel.

The faith of the people of Israel has often been referred to as a national religion, but this is quite misleading. It cannot be labelled national in the sense that it stems from one state or political institution, for only for the comparatively short period of the reigns of David and Solomon was the people of Israel contained within one kingdom. For a somewhat longer period there were two kingdoms. But for by far the longest period, Israel possessed no political institution which gave her an independent national existence. That which enabled Israel to survive as a community, even though dispersed among the nations, was the common faith. As the community of faith, Israel pioneered the Christian Way.

Neither can Israel's faith be called a national religion on the grounds that she was one pure ethnic group, for as we have already pointed out, the Israel of David's kingdom was much more cosmopolitan than is usually realized. It is true that in the course of time it gave the appearance of being a national group, for many generations went by, in which little new blood, if any at all, was brought in to share the faith. But it is salutary for us to remember, that to the Indian and Chinese of the nineteenth century, Christianity had all the appearances of being the religion of the European race.

When the Jewish remnant of Israel became scattered through various nations and cultures which were alien to it, it led to two opposite kinds of reaction. The more dominant trend was to develop self-contained Jewish communities which existed like islands in a sea of alien culture. This concern for self-preservation fostered the inward look, leading to restrictions forbidding marriage outside the community, an emphasis on all customs unique to the Jewish faith, and strict laws of food and hygiene which prevented Jews from having table fellowship with Gentiles.

But there were some men in Judaism who protested against this. They looked outward, and believed that their faith led them to a sense of responsibility for the whole race of mankind. This concern found expression in the late Old Testament books of Ruth and Jonah, though there were seeds of it in Israel's earliest traditions, such as the divine words spoken to Abraham, "By you all the families of the earth will bless themselves".

A contemporary of Jesus was the great Jewish philosopher Philo (c. 20 B.C.– c. A.D. 50), who attempted to interpret the Jewish faith to the Gentile world in such a way as to solicit the interest and appreciation of non-Jewish readers. The Pharisees definitely set out to make converts to Judaism. Indeed, not long before, the Idumeans (the descendants of ancient Edom), from whom the Herods came, were induced by force to embrace the Jewish faith and practice. Such examples show that Judaism was not simply an ethnic or national faith, but a community of faith which still occasionally looked outward.

This catholic or universal interest, which meant all the difference between a community of faith and a religion of race or state, was destined to break out in an astounding way as a result of the advent of Christ. But it did not happen straight away. It is widely accepted nowadays that Jesus had no thought of founding a church embodying all the ecclesiastical structure that we associate with the word. He probably never used the word 'church', for the only two references found on his lips in the Gospels almost certainly reflect later tradition. We have already noted the probability that Jesus expected the end of the age within a short time. Moreover, not even the Gospels set on the lips of the earthly Jesus any hint of a mission to men outside Jewry, but they record him as saying that he came to the lost sheep of the house of Israel.

It was largely due to Paul that the Christian movement began to move outside the boundaries of Jewry, and this partly derived from the discovery that, whereas there was considerable resistance among the Jews to the new form of the faith, some of the Gentile adherents of the various synagogue centres were quickly attracted to the Christian Gospel. When Jewish resistance turned to fierce opposition on the missionary journey to the synagogues of Asia Minor, Paul and Barnabas finally announced to their Jewish compatriots the following decision, which had such momentous results: "It was necessary that the word of God should be spoken first to you. Since you thrust it from you, and judge yourselves unworthy of eternal life, behold, we turn to the Gentiles".

The earliest Christians, being themselves Jews and centred in Jerusalem, were not a little alarmed when they found that the Gentile converts were not being made to conform to orthodox Jewish practice, and the Christian movement almost split in two over the issue. Eventually an agreement was reached that Paul and Barnabas should be free to take the Gospel to the Gentiles, and that the original apostles James, Peter and John should preach to the Jews. The famous missionary injunctions in the Gospels and Acts, such as, "Go therefore and make disciples of all nations . . ." are all placed on the lips of the risen Jesus, the Christ of faith, and reflect what began to happen only ten to twenty years after the death of Jesus.

It was this dramatic move, initiated by Paul in obedience to what he believed to be divine direction, which was crucial for the future of Christianity, and without which the world may never have heard of the Christian faith. It was crucial because it allowed to come to the fore the heart and essence of the Judeo-Christian faith. For Christianity is essentially a faith to be lived. It expresses itself in the lives of those who embrace it and in the community of faith which together they constitute. From this point onwards

Christianity left behind the security of the institutional structures of temple and synagogue. It went out into the world to sink or swim. It had so little framework or organization to hold it together that it could easily have faded out (and perhaps it did in some places), but on the whole it did just the opposite. It spread with the vitality of fire.

We have already noted earlier that when compared with the commonly accepted religious practices of the day, the Christian community of faith took on an everyday, almost secular appearance, not unlike such a contemporary movement as the Rotarians. There were no priests, no paid officials, no uniformity of practice and the bare minimum of organization. But the vital things were found there unencumbered—a common faith, a living hope and a new level of love. Honesty, purity, gentleness, patience, love were fostered in the whole of life, not simply to make a good impression upon others, but because these were the only proper expression of the faith they had embraced. They were the fruits of what they found to be the power of God in the community of faith.

Jesus had founded no church of the kind that we know. But he had spoken consistently of the Kingdom of God, or the rule of God in the lives of men. Much of the original teaching of Jesus seems to have consisted of the parables of the Kingdom, which highlighted various aspects of the life of the community of faith. Let us take, for example, the parable in which Jesus likened the Kingdom of God to the leaven which a housewife puts into the flour to make bread. The leaven has to lose its independent identity in the flour, but by spreading throughout the whole, it slowly turns the flour into the living, fermenting dough ready to be baked into bread.

In the first place this describes how faith works in the life of the believer. When a man embraces the faith, there may be nothing at first that is very obvious to an outside observer, but Christian faith, like leaven, spreads through a man's whole being, influencing in the end all his thinking and action. In the second place, the community of faith is not a separatist closed circle of self-satisfied members living to themselves, but a community which is again and again prepared to lose its own identity, that, like leaven, it may come to influence the whole of human society in which it lives.

Of course, we look back to the first Christian century through spectacles which have been ground and coloured by some sixteen hundred years of the history of the church as an institution co-extensive with the state. Until the beginning of the fourth century the Christian movement had been forced from time to time to live an underground existence, owing to the imperial persecutions, but

Constantine the Great, partly in the belief that the Christian God had given him the victory over his rival contestants for the Empire, not only gave complete freedom to Christians for the practice of the faith, but he united the Christian church to the secular state by quite close ties.

In the course of time the church developed an ever stronger framework of organization, a more formal expression of doctrine, and an intricate liturgical cultus. This reached a climax in the Middle Ages, by which time the church had in her hands social power stronger than that of kings and emperors. On the one hand we can be strongly attracted by the magnificent features of the Middle Ages, as an inspiring expression of the Christian faith in a certain age and place. On the other hand, it is all too easy from our vantage point to behold those faults in the edifice of medieval Christendom which were destined in the long run to bring the whole intricate structure into increasing decay. There is no more telling commentary on this, than a visit to one of the medieval cathedrals, usually empty, with the all too obvious signs of decay, and the inevitable appeal for funds to help restore it.

But when Christianity takes to itself the forms and organization of the kingdoms of this world, it must expect that these structures will suffer the same fate as those of man-made empires, even if they are Christian in intention. The Reformation was the first great crack in the structure, though it had already been preceded by the break between East and West. In some respects at least, the Reformers were making a move in the right direction. They were challenging the rigid structure of the church, in which decay had already set in, in order to give breathing space to the essentially living thing that the Christian faith is. But it was no more than a temporary burst forward, for the Reformers only partially diagnosed what was happening. The various churches of Protestantism quickly set up their own rigid counterparts of the ecclesiastical structure centred on Rome, and were still intent, though sometimes unconsciously, on preserving as much of the institutional form of Christendom as they could.

But the door that the Reformers opened, let in more things than they bargained for. The new world began to emerge, though at first very few, if any at all, had any inkling of this. The leaven of the Christian heritage now began to penetrate further than either Protestant or Catholic realized, and in forms which could not readily be evaluated by the traditional canons of Christian orthodoxy. The emergence of the new world, which in fact owed so much to the Christian heritage, began to appear more and more in the eyes of the authorities of Christendom as an evil spirit from some Pandora's box.

Steadily over the last two hundred years, and with increasing acceleration during this century, the remnants of eastern and western Christianity, of both Protestant and Catholic forms, have been forced back into themselves. Churchmen of various traditions are making strenuous efforts to prevent the once magnificent edifice of Christendom from falling into further ruin. The churches have become island organizations living within a sea of increasingly secular society. It is not the first time that the community of faith has become inward looking. Some, like the ancient Sadducees, are content to carry on with their priestly tasks regardless. Others, like the ancient Pharisees, prompted by equally noble motives, are making valiant efforts to keep the church structures buoyant and active by winning converts from the lost world as occasion offers.

Within the last hundred years the rise of the ecumenical movement has brought new hope to many, and much that it seeks to do deserves the fullest support. But what appears to be the ecumenical diagnosis, namely, that the trouble with the church lies in her divisions, does not go far enough. Lurking behind most ecumenical endeavours there seems to lie the vision of restoring the magnificence of European Christendom, though this time on a global scale. But the Middle Ages have gone for ever. There can be no restoring of the edifice by plastering over the cracks in the masonry. The medieval cathedrals are destined to become museum-pieces, just as much in Europe, as they are in Russia. The whole ecclesiastical structure is destined to undergo a much greater shaking yet.

In fact, the church as it has been known to us through European Christendom is destined to die, and we must let it die. For only then can there be a resurrection of the community of faith in a form relevant to the new world. It was the death of the Davidic kingdom which forced the Jewish community of faith out into the world. It was the death of Christ which led to the renewal of the community of faith. It was the dying to the old social structure of temple and synagogue which gave a freedom to the Christian community to spread out into the Roman world. The present decay of traditional Christendom is a challenge to our faith in death and resurrection.

We are unwilling and afraid to let the outworn organization, doctrine, and forms of the church die, lest we find in the end that we have nothing left. Herein we reveal our lack of faith. That which is permanent in the church is not its structure, its doctrinal confessions and its liturgies, but its faith, and the hope and love associated with it. The more faith becomes a present experience, the more we are willing to let the outward forms of past generations die, that the living church may show itself for what it is—the community of faith.

Of course every human community must assume some kind of form, however loose and impermanent the framework may be. At the moment we cannot see clearly what form the community of faith will take in the new world, say by next century, any more than Paul could have foreseen the great church of Christendom which was destined to develop from the church of his time. But because the church must learn to be the community of faith, we must abandon the idea of the church as an institution of power. How often we are still tempted to bring influence to bear upon secular powers by calling on the church to speak with some kind of authority through its leaders and councils. The church is not called to be an institution within society, but to be the leaven of society. The real influence of the community of faith will not be through the power of the institution but through the lives of its members, and there will never be any easy way of evaluating this influence.

The recovery of the church as the community of faith will not come out of the blue, but out of the existing, fragmented and outwardly dying ecclesiastical institutions of Christendom. The denominational barriers are collapsing. Men of faith from all traditions are entering into honest dialogue not only with one another, but also with those who have abandoned traditional Christianity of any form. New life is breaking out from the churches in unexpected ways. These are the encouraging signs, that from the decaying structure of medieval Christendom there is beginning to emerge the new form of the church as the community of faith, whose role it is to serve all mankind by being the leaven of faith, hope and love in a distressed world.

CHAPTER 21

The Faith which Outlives Death

We have made an attempt to show the meaning of Christian faith in the new world, by sketching it in terms of faith, hope and love. Because we are thinking creatures we naturally search for meaning and purpose in the life we find ourselves living in this world, and nothing can be meaningful unless we are able to understand it, at least to some degree. The discussion of the nature and relevance of the Christian faith therefore always plays some part in bringing us into encounter with that deepest reality in life we call God.

But writing and reading about the nature of the faith can never take the place of the life of faith itself. As we have said before, Christian faith is essentially to be lived and experienced. There will never be any complete or ultimate form of verbal expression into which it can be translated. Man will never reach the point where he has spoken the last word about it, and indeed no believer ever understands anything like the whole of it. Because man is a creature of history, his experience of faith will inevitably be expressed in words and terms which reflect the character of his time and cultural condition. Because each man is limited in his experience, his expression of his faith will also be limited and piecemeal.

Since faith is a personal experience, it means that it is only the man of faith who can talk about it at all in any real way. At first this may sound somewhat arrogant, but a moment's reflection soon makes it clear that this is true of all kinds of personal experiences. Only a person who has experienced pain can begin to attempt to describe it, and it is impossible to communicate the experience adequately in words to a person who has never experienced any pain at all. Only a person who has had sight can talk about what it means to be able to see. So with faith, as with pain and sight, words alone are insufficient in themselves to convince the unbeliever about the reality of faith.

There will always be obstacles to faith, which no amount of discussion and explanation can surmount, and there always have been. They can all be described as the demand for more convincing proof, and strangely enough they come from two quite different directions, both of which were already known in the first century. Paul spoke of them when he said, "Jews demand signs and Greeks seek wisdom." The Jew was a religionist who believed he already possessed a sure sign from God, and he was unwilling to move out in faith from this sign until he received another. He wanted to avoid the life of faith by moving from one sure sign to another, just as the learner-swimmer wants to move through the pool with his hand on one rail after another. There are religionists today who think they already possess a sure sign from God, in an authoritative church or an infallible Bible, and they are unwilling to surrender this security and venture out in faith. The appeal to a certain sign becomes a stumbling-block to faith today as it did for the ancient Jew.

But the Greek demanded a convincing argument, and until he received it, he too refused to make the venture of faith. There are men today who look at Christianity from the outside, read about it, turn it over in their minds, and still stand aloof, waiting for it to be presented as a logical and convincing piece of argument. To them it seems foolish to commit oneself to Christianity, when it is not capable of rational proof. But of course it is just because there is no rational answer to the meaning of life, that man is forced to live by faith. And in doing so, he finds in the end that faith is the very spice of human existence.

In all forms of faith there must be some acts of trust, great or small, but in the Christian faith it is an act of commitment followed by a continuing sense of commitment, which makes the difference between faith and unbelief. As the person who is unwilling to take the plunge into the water will never learn to swim, so the man who holds back from commitment to the Christian heritage cannot hope to learn what it means to live by Christian faith.

The life of faith makes itself manifest in the kind of decision and the quality of action, which the believer makes in all the events of life in which he is involved. Sometimes the first act of commitment is more dramatic than any others which follow, and the believer looks back to it in gratitude as a turning point in his life. But often the origins of the life of faith cannot be clearly discerned and remembered at all, for it has grown out of a long series of decisions and acts of trust. In any case, the life of faith is being daily challenged and tested afresh in the decisions and crises, both great and small, of which normal life consists.

We shall now attempt to describe the life of faith from the inside. It is important to remember that this is a description in the language of faith, and not an attempt to discuss its validity. Although there are certain basic forms which are common to nearly all Christians, such as, "I believe in God through Jesus Christ our Lord and Saviour", no two Christians would describe the experience of the life of faith in exactly the same terms. Not only must the uniqueness of each man be taken into account, but also the diversity of cultural background, personal experience, educational attainment and intellectual level of comprehension.

If God is the deepest reality for human existence, then He must speak to all men, in all their diversity, but the way in which the faith created by His word comes to be expressed by the believer, will vary considerably. Some take the step of faith using a mental conception of God which is more concrete in outline, and even more man-shaped, than some others would find meaningful. Some form a mental image of the Christ of faith which is more imaginative and picturesque than others would allow. One of the reasons why the community of faith has long been known as catholic or universal, is that it must hold together in love and mutual respect all the diversity that our individuality brings to the experience of faith.

The first thing to be said is this. Even though the believer has been consciously looking for something to satisfy his longings, and searching for some purpose in life, his embracing of the Christian faith does not mean that at last he has found what he is looking for, so much as the strange conviction that he has himself been found. Like the men of old to whom the Bible bears witness, such as Moses and Jeremiah, Peter and Andrew, who found themselves unexpectedly called, so the Christian is one who has found himself challenged by the community of faith and the Gospel it proclaims. The challenge has come to him as the very Word of God.

This Word may have come in any of many ways. There is usually nothing very dramatic about it. It is a Word which is heard in the inner ear, and at first the Christian may have tried to evade it. But the Word of God has an insistence about it that does not let men go readily. Yet on the other hand the Word does not trespass on a man's own integrity. It does not take away from man the power of choice. God does not manifest Himself in all His strength, and, by showing up man in all his weakness, force him into submission. Rather it is a case of man, in spite of all *his* strength, being encountered by God in *His* weakness. The ancient prophet Elijah made a pilgrimage to the holy mountain of God and looked for God in the tornado, the earthquake and the fire. But the Word of God came to him in the weakness of a 'still small voice'.

And the voice said "What are you doing here, Elijah?" That illustrates the second point. The Word of God that comes to men through the Christian heritage calls them to decision. The particular act which may initiate the life of faith and obedience is only the first of a whole series, for the Christian life is one which is consciously lived in obedience. A Christian is one who is very much aware of the fact that he is not his own master, if indeed he ever has been. Now he knows himself as a servant. He is not here in this world to please himself, to achieve his own ambitions, or to plan his own way ahead. He is here to serve and it is in service that he finds his freedom.

It is the life of obedience which gives meaning and direction to his life. He is no longer meandering blindly along. And because he now has a purpose, he finds a new zest in living and a new power to make progress on the way and to get things done. It is not the kind of obedience, however, which takes from him the need to think and make decisions, as it would be, perhaps, if he had become enslaved to a fellowman. Although he has given himself in obedience, there is the need to cultivate the attentive ear to hear the word of direction. In the Christian heritage, there are guidelines which help him in discerning the word of God, but there is no foolproof method of being absolutely sure. In faith, and in a certain amount of tension, he must learn steadily to grow more sensitive to the leading that he expects.

But what is the source of this Word? To whom has he committed himself in obedience? The Christian does not know. It is only in the language of faith that he can answer. The Christian believes that He who spoke to Moses and the prophets, and whose very Word became flesh in the man Jesus, is the One who addresses him and calls him to obedience. If the Christian is asked to prove or demonstrate the validity of his belief, he cannot do so. He recognizes that though there may have been a particular factor in the life of the church, or in the Bible, or in some rational argument which carried a lot of weight with him, none of these proves anything in the end. Nevertheless, the fact that the call to obedience rests upon faith alone, does not take away from the Christian the sense of reality he has found in the life of daily obedience.

The life of obedience is usually felt to be one involving a personal relationship. The Christian usually speaks in personal terms about God, the source of the Word by which he has been addressed and which he seeks to obey, but he freely confesses that the reality pointed to by this word is quite beyond his knowledge and comprehension. What gives him confidence in his conviction is not any esoteric knowledge of the mysterious God which has been revealed to him, but the testimony of the Bible and of the community of faith to the great company of people who in their own day believed they heard the Word of the same God and sought to obey.

But though God, as the deepest reality of the universe, remains beyond man's grasp, the Christian has a tangible point of reference. The God whose Word he hears and seeks to obey, is the God who spoke through the human scene in a way which culminated in the advent of the man Jesus. The Christian sees in the man Jesus the clearest representation of God. Yet even the man Jesus is not tangible for the believer, and never has been, for it was only subsequent to the earthly life of Jesus, that Christian faith was focussed upon the risen Jesus as the Christ of faith.

In directing attention to the Christ of faith, the community of faith has traditionally spoken in terms of Incarnation, the Word of God become flesh. Paul described Christ as one who "emptied himself, taking the form of a servant, being born in the likeness of men. And being found in human form he humbled himself and became obedient unto death, even death on a cross." We have already seen earlier how the advent of Jesus Christ became the culminating point of Israel's concern with the historical human scene. The affirmation that the Word of God has finally become man calls upon man to accept his own humanity and to abandon all mythological pretensions to be an immortal god. For the God of Israel Himself has done just this. He has emptied Himself of all mythological divinity and become man. In this act, humanity is raised to a new dignity and honour, and its full potential comes to realization.

Thus in the life of obedient faith, the Christian fastens his attention upon the Christ of faith as the focal point of the whole Christian heritage. The man Jesus at one and the same time shows us the full potential in man, and brings us into encounter with God, the deepest reality for our existence. And at the centre of the Christ faith is the basic symbol of Christianity, the cross. The community of faith has rightly never forgotten that Jesus was crucified, and has been convinced that this was no accident. The man Jesus would not have become the Christ of faith, if he had not been crucified, or at least taken death upon Himself in some similar way.

The Christian has found in the cross the key to the problem of the tragic element of evil which comes to light in man's inhumanity to man, war, oppression, hatred, greed and famine. Man's attempt to save himself from the tragedy of life only serves to accentuate the problem, for it largely arose in the first place from man's self-concern, self-will and self-centredness. In fact it is not in man to save himself. The cross shows, however, that by surrendering himself, he can be used to save others. "He saved others; he cannot save himself", was the Word of God which came from the very mouths of mockers.

The conviction that the key to the renewal of the human situation is to be found in the surrender of the self, the surrender of personal hopes and ambitions, and the obedient commitment of oneself to live in love for the needs of others, is not something which man has in fact found out by himself. Man has been led to it by the developing heritage. The way was already being prepared by God when He called to selfless obedience men of Israel such as Moses, Elijah, Hosea and Jeremiah. It became more clearly defined in the words of the unknown prophet of Israel, who outlined the role of the true servant of YHWH as one who took suffering upon himself voluntarily:

> But he was wounded for our transgressions,
> he was bruised for our iniquities . . .
> he was oppressed, and he was afflicted,
> yet he opened not his mouth . . .
> he was cut off out of the land of the living,
> stricken for the transgression of my people . . .
> although he had done no violence,
> and there was no deceit in his mouth . . .
> he poured out his soul to death,
> and was numbered with the transgressors.

The Christian sees this role of selfless suffering brought to a consummation in the crucifixion of Jesus. Because he finds there the key to the element of tragedy in human existence, the cross becomes the chief point of encounter with God, and from it he hears the challenge of Jesus as the very Word of God, "If any man would come after me, let him deny himself and take up his cross and follow me". The symbol of the cross holds up before the Christian the choice before him in the decisions to be made in each new day of life. Is he to turn sorrowfully away because he has rich possessions, high hopes of his own and secret ambitions? Or is he to surrender all these pretensions and aspirations for himself either in this mortal life or beyond death?

To take up the cross means to prepare oneself to die, to die completely. This is the path which Jesus chose and which he trod voluntarily. His death on the cross has often been gravely travestied by well-meaning Christians when they imagined that he faced the cross with the secret knowledge that less than thirty-six hours later he would be alive again and ready to ascend into heaven. This makes a mockery of the cross. Jesus was ready to die, really to die. This is the kind of cross to which he calls his followers.

He who is ready to surrender his hopes, ambitions, and life itself, for the love of God and his fellowmen, no longer fears death and the end of human existence, for that self-centred concern which wants to cling on to life beyond its appointed span, and seeks to bring it back again in some supernatural realm, has already died.

The Christian is still keenly aware of the tragedy of human life, and the limitations in which his mortality involves him, but death no longer holds any fears for him. Christian faith takes the sting out of death, and makes even death subservient to the cause of life and the renewal of mankind.

There is one final point. It can be mentioned only at the end, and even then in some ways it should only be whispered, lest it be regarded as a kind of reward for those who shoulder the cross. When this happens, the real significance of the cross tends to be lost sight of. The Christian is called to the way of the cross not for any self-gain either in this life or beyond death, but simply and solely out of the love of God and one's fellows.

But there is no keeping of this point secret, for though it is full of mystery it has been the chief source of joy and wonder in Christian experience. It took the first disciples, we are told, completely by surprise. Jesus was dead. Yet they found him more alive than ever. They spoke of it in terms of resurrection and they rejoiced. They were given the courage to shoulder their own crosses and become witnesses or martyrs, and new life rose within them. It was the life of Christ. Paul put it in a nutshell, "I have been crucified with Christ; it is no longer I who live, but Christ who lives in me."

The Christian who commits himself to Christ as Lord, and voluntarily takes upon himself the way of the cross, also knows something of the unexpected joy of the resurrection. He finds that though he has put an end (as he thought) to the personal ambitions which appeared to make life interesting, to his surprise there is welling up within him a new source of life. It brings to him a stronger faith, a clearer hope, a more vibrant love. Life takes on for him a new quality, a quality that justifies the name eternal. In submitting himself to the life of obedience, in seeking to be used as an instrument in the renewal of the world, in shouldering the cross of Christ his Lord, the Christian shares in the life of that faith which genuinely *outlives* death. There is much that he does not understand. He has no sure knowledge of the eternal verities, but he holds them by faith, and looks in faith to the God whose Word of life he has heard in the man Jesus and he says:

> Good Lord, teach us to serve you as you deserve,
> to give and not to count the cost,
> to fight and not to heed the wounds,
> to toil and not to seek for rest,
> to labour and not to ask for any reward,
> save that of knowing that we do your will,
> through Jesus Christ our Lord.

Suggestions for Further Reading

PART I

John Dillenberger, *Protestant Thought and Natural Science*, Collins
J. D. Smart, *The Interpretation of Scripture*, S.C.M. Press
Alan Richardson, *The Bible in the Age of Science*, S.C.M. Press
J. S. Habgood, *Religion and Science*, Mills & Boon
C. F. von Weizsäcker, *The Relevance of Science*, Collins
Gustav Schenk, *The History of Man*, Weidenfeld & Nicolson
Harvey Cox, *The Secular City*, S.C.M. Press
John A. T. Robinson, *The New Reformation*, S.C.M. Press

PART II

Henri Frankfort and others, *Before Philosophy*, Penguin
Claus Westermann, *A Thousand Years and a Day*, S.C.M. Press
T. J. Meek, *Hebrew Origins*, Harper
B. W. Anderson, *The Living World of the Old Testament*, Longmans
Rudolf Bultmann, *Jesus Christ and Mythology*, S.C.M. Press
Gerhard Gloege, *The Day of His Coming*, S.C.M. Press
Heinz Zahrnt, *The Historical Jesus*, Collins
Günther Bornkamm, *Jesus of Nazareth*, Hodder & Stoughton
James McLeman, *Jesus in our Time*, Hodder & Stoughton
H. H. Rex, *Did Jesus rise from the Dead?* Blackwood & Janet Paul Ltd

PART III

John Knox, *Myth and Truth*, Carey Kingsgate Press Ltd
Dietrich Bonhoeffer, *Letters and Papers from Prison*, Collins
Lesslie Newbigin, *Honest Religion for Secular Man*, S.C.M. Press
Alan Richardson, *Religion in Contemporary Debate*, S.C.M. Press
F. C. Happold, *Religious Faith and Twentieth Century Man*, Penguin
Nathaniel Micklem, *A Religion for Agnostics*, S.C.M. Press
Paul Tillich, *The Shaking of the Foundations*, Penguin
R. Gregor Smith, *Secular Christianity*, Collins
Thomas W. Ogletree, *The "Death of God" Controversy*, S.C.M. Press

Alfred B. Starratt, *The Real God*, S.C.M. Press
Daniel Jenkins, *Beyond Religion*, S.C.M. Press
David Jenkins, *Guide to the Debate About God*, Lutterworth Press
W. Hordern, *Speaking of God*, Epworth Press
Peter L. Berger, *The Noise of Solemn Assemblies*, Doubleday

Index